The FDR Way

GREAT *Presidential* DECISIONS

The **FDR** Way

JEFFREY MORRIS

LERNER PUBLICATIONS COMPANY
MINNEAPOLIS

To Mat and Jeannie, Josh and Ben,
who set the standards for friendship

Library of Congress Cataloging-in-Publication Data

Morris, Jeffrey Brandon, 1941–
    The FDR way / Jeffrey B. Morris.
        p. cm. — (Great presidential decisions)
    Includes index.
    Summary: Discusses the life and presidency of Franklin
Delano Roosevelt, with an emphasis on the important
decisions he made in that office regarding the American
banking system, social security, the Supreme Court,
World War II, and the United Nations, among others.
    ISBN 0-8225-2929-7 (alk. paper)
    1. Roosevelt, Franklin D. (Franklin Delano), 1882–1945—
Juvenile literature. 2. United States—Politics and
government—1933–1945—Decision making—Juvenile
literature. 3. Decision-making—United States—History—
20th century—Juvenile literature. 4. Presidents—United
States—Biography—Juvenile literature. [1. Roosevelt,
Franklin D. (Franklin Delano) 1882–1945. 2. Presidents.
3. United States—Politics and government—1933–1945.
4. Decision making.] I. Title. II. Series.
E807.M79 1995
973.917'092—dc20
[B]   95-12575

Manufactured in the United States of America

1 2 3 4 5 6 – JR – 01 00 99 98 97 96

Contents

Introduction

*T*HE FRAMERS OF THE UNITED States Constitution created a complicated form of government. They divided the powers of the U.S. government among three branches. They thought that the least powerful branch would be the judiciary. That branch was supposed to hear and decide lawsuits, decide disputes between the U.S. government and the individual states, and keep the other two branches within their constitutional powers. The framers expected that the Congress would become the most powerful branch, because it was supposed to make laws, levy taxes, and choose how to spend money.

The framers of the Constitution had the most trouble agreeing on the powers of the head of the executive branch. They needed to create an official who could act speedily and forcefully. On the other hand, they definitely did not want a king or

In 1787 George Washington presided over the Constitutional Convention in Philadelphia, where he and his fellow delegates hammered out a remarkable new form of government.

7

We the People

The Constitution begins "We the people," showing that the American government is elected by the people and is responsible to them.

dictator. Finally, they agreed to create the office of president. The president would be elected for four years. He or she would be commander in chief of the military forces, would be primarily responsible for relations with other countries, and have the duty of seeing that the laws passed by Congress would be carried out.

The framers knew that each branch would work at a different rate of speed because they would have different things to do. The judicial branch would act most slowly, partly because the need for fairness in court requires it and partly because lawyers usually take time to do their jobs.

The Congress would probably also act relatively slowly, partly because of the need to get agreement among its many members and partly

because members of legislative bodies like to give speeches. The framers, however, wanted the president to be able to act rapidly and decisively. When they drafted the Constitution, the framers expected that the Supreme Court would only meet at the nation's capital a few weeks out of the year. But they intended that the president, even if he or she was away from the capital, should act for the nation in an emergency.

The framers also wanted to be sure that in some areas—such as in war and in dealing with other countries—this nation would be as unified as possible, and they hoped that the president could express that unity. For these reasons, therefore, for speed, unity, and because he or she would always be ready to act in an emergency, the framers expected that the president would often be called upon to make important decisions.

These books are about the great decisions made by our presidents. Of course, presidents make decisions every day. They decide whom to appoint to

Among the framers of the Constitution were *(left to right)* Alexander Hamilton, James Madison, Charles Cotesworth Pinckney, Benjamin Franklin, Roger Sherman, and Elbridge Gerry.

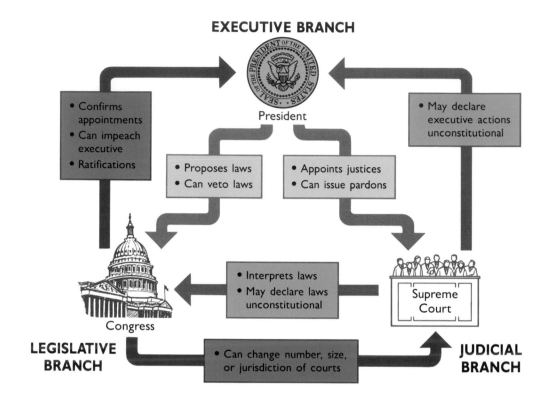

EXECUTIVE BRANCH

President

- Confirms appointments
- Can impeach executive
- Ratifications

- May declare executive actions unconstitutional

- Proposes laws
- Can veto laws

- Appoints justices
- Can issue pardons

- Interprets laws
- May declare laws unconstitutional

Congress

Supreme Court

LEGISLATIVE BRANCH

- Can change number, size, or jurisdiction of courts

JUDICIAL BRANCH

office, what to say to leaders of foreign nations, whether or not to veto laws of Congress. Most of these decisions are quite ordinary. From time to time, however, the president makes a decision which will affect the American people (and maybe other nations as well) for many years, maybe even centuries. You may think of Lincoln's decision to free the slaves, or Truman's to contain Communism, or Kennedy's decision to fight for the civil rights of African Americans. Of course, not every important decision our presidents have made has been wise. James Buchanan decided not to stop the southern states from leaving the Union. Lyndon B. Johnson decided to escalate the war in Vietnam. Richard Nixon decided to cover up the Watergate burglary.

In these books we will try to learn about some of the presidents who have made important decisions and about some of those decisions. We will look at what led up to the decision, the choices the president had, and how the president actually went about making the decision. We will also look to see how the decision was carried out and why the decision was important.

This book is about Franklin Delano Roosevelt and the decisions he made as president. Roosevelt (known to the American people as "FDR") was president for twelve years, longer than anyone else. Elected to four terms (he died early in his fourth term), Roosevelt served during two of the greatest crises in American history—the Great Depression and World War II.

Deciding which of Roosevelt's decisions to write about was not easy. Six have been chosen: his decision to fight the Depression with all the powers of the United States government; his decision to fight for passage of the Social Security Act; his decision to try to get Congress to increase the size of the Supreme Court; his decision to aid Great Britain at the time of its greatest peril from Nazi Germany; his decision to run for a third term; and his decision during World War II to work toward the creation of the United Nations.

To cover all of Roosevelt's major decisions would have meant writing a book three times the size of this one. But by studying the decisions covered here, you will see why historians agree that Roosevelt changed the United States more than any other president of the twentieth century.

*T*he American flag and the Great Seal both symbolize American values. In the Great Seal, the eagle holds both an olive branch and arrows, reminding us that the United States desires peace but will wage war if necessary.

CHAPTER
ONE

A Country in Crisis

EVER IN THE HISTORY OF THE United States—the land of opportunity— had there been such misery as in the days and months leading to Franklin Roosevelt's first inauguration on March 4, 1933. Thirteen million people were out of work, perhaps one-quarter of the working population. No town or city was spared. Businesses and banks closed. Even some schools had to close temporarily because state governments didn't have enough money to pay teachers. Half of America's farmers were on the brink of losing their farms, unable to pay their mortgages. No other depression in U.S. history lasted so long or caused as much grief as the one called the "Great Depression."

During the Great Depression, soup kitchens fed millions of hungry, unemployed Americans.

This 1937 painting of jobless people seeking work conveys the despair caused by the Depression.

The Great Depression is often said to have begun with a terrible drop in the stock market in October 1929—although farmers had been having very hard times before that. The market continued to drop and millions of investors lost their life savings. Within three years national income dropped from $80 billion to $38 billion. Even the farmers who had not lost their farms were too poor to buy manufactured goods. Between 1930 and 1933 more than 5,500 banks closed and millions of savings accounts were wiped out.

By 1932, U.S. manufacturing production had

dropped to $31 billion from $70 billion in 1929. The production of steel dropped to one-fifth the capacity of the industry. United States Steel, which had employed 225,000 full-time workers in 1929, did not employ any full-time workers four years later. By 1933, one out of every four American workers had lost his or her job and a large percentage of those who were still working received such low wages or worked so few hours that they could barely survive. One hundred thousand businesses failed. Millions lost their life savings in the stock market or because of bank failures. More than 1,000 homes were foreclosed on every day. A complete collapse of the national economy seemed inevitable.

In 1932, farmers—who had been suffering for at least a decade before the Great Depression—had their smallest cash incomes in 25 years. Prices were so low that many farmers let their crops rot in the fields because it didn't pay to ship them to market. Perhaps as many as one-third of American farmers had already lost their farms because they couldn't pay the mortgages. Countless others had simply abandoned their farms.

The nation's misery was visible. Thousands of families lost their homes. The country was dotted with "Hoovervilles"—clusters of tar-paper huts roofed with tin cans named for President Herbert Hoover, who had been unsuccessful in fighting the Depression during his administration. A Hooverville in New York City stretched for two miles along the Hudson River. One couple lived in a cave in Central Park. In Los Angeles, many of those who could not pay their heating bills cooked outside over

Migrant workers journeyed to California from drought-stricken sections of the South and Southwest in search of work. These shacks were part of a road-side settlement of migrant workers in the commercial pea district of the San Joaquin Valley in California.

wood fires. In Chicago, 50 men fought over a barrel of garbage outside a restaurant. In every city, men and women waited in long lines for rations of bread.

When Franklin Roosevelt became president on March 4, 1933, the Depression showed no signs of hitting bottom. In fact, things were getting worse. In the month before Roosevelt took office, America's banking system had collapsed. After *all* the banks in Detroit closed for eight days—leaving 900,000 depositors unable to use their money—millions of Americans became concerned that they would lose their life savings. People—holding paper bags for their money—formed long lines in front of banks throughout the United States. They thought their money would be safer in old shoe boxes and under mattresses. But the banks did not have enough money to give every depositor his or her money

immediately. State after state began proclaiming bank "holidays," temporarily closing the banks. By March 4, 1933, banks were temporarily closed in all but two states, as were markets for the sale of stocks and grain. The American economy had fallen apart.

The United States government had not been able to do anything to end the Depression. Congress met between December 1932 and February 1933, but was unable to pass a single important law to help the economy. Without strong presidential leadership, unsure of what to do next, Congress spent its time dealing with minor matters. President Hoover said, "We are at the end of our string." Many believed that if the federal government couldn't deal effectively with the widespread suffering, democracy itself would be in peril. There were incidents of smashed store windows, freight trains forced to halt,

The Depression affected rural as well as urban areas. These children lived near Vicksburg, Mississippi.

On March 4, 1933, Chief Justice Charles Evans Hughes *(right)* administered the oath of office to FDR.

and violence used to prevent court-ordered sales of farms. On the day of Roosevelt's inauguration, hunger marchers paraded in New York City and Chicago.

On March 4, 1933, a despairing nation awaited its new president. It was not a nice day in Washington. A chill wind blew from the northwest, bringing gusts of rain. Nevertheless, a crowd of 100,000 waited at the Capitol for the inaugural ceremony. The outgoing president, Herbert Hoover, and the new one, Franklin Roosevelt, rode to the Capitol in silence. The new vice president, John Nance Garner, took his oath of office inside the Capitol. Then Roosevelt, handicapped by polio, walked slowly down a ramp on the arm of his son James. On a platform outside the Capitol, the magnificently bearded chief justice, Charles Evans

Hughes, read the oath of office, which Roosevelt repeated.

Unsmiling, Roosevelt began to speak—not only to the crowd in front of him, but to the millions who listened over the radio. His speech may have been the most effective inaugural address ever given. He began by stating that this was "the time to speak the truth, the whole truth, frankly and boldly." He urged his listeners not to "shrink from honestly facing conditions in our country today." Roosevelt went on to say, "This great nation will endure as it has endured, will revive and prosper." He asked the American people to summon all of their courage:

> Let me assert my firm belief that the only thing we have to fear is fear itself—nameless, unreasoning, unjustified terror which paralyzes needed efforts to convert retreat into advance.

"The nation asks for action, and action now," Roosevelt said—action to put people to work. Roosevelt closed by asking the blessing of God and telling his listeners that he trusted the future of democracy. The American people had asked him to act, and he was ready to do so.

Only when he was done and the applause began did he smile—"a great, wide, joyous, confident smile." In this way, Franklin Delano Roosevelt, thirty-second president of the United States, began the first of his four terms.

A Life of Privilege and Pain

FOR 40 YEARS, FRANKLIN DELANO Roosevelt had lived a life all of us might envy. Then tragedy struck. For the rest of his life, he could not get out of bed, sit in a chair, or leave a room without help.

Roosevelt was of Dutch and English ancestry. The first Roosevelt to live in America, Klaes Martensen van Roosevelt, had settled in New York City in 1645. FDR's parents had both come from wealthy families. His father, James, was the vice president of the Delaware and Hudson Railway Company.

Franklin was born on January 30, 1882, at Hyde Park, his parent's magnificent estate about 100 miles north of New York City. The house commanded a breathtaking view of the Hudson River and the

Young FDR with his parents, Sara and James, on the south lawn of their Hyde Park, New York, estate.

Catskill Mountains. The estate, 100 acres in size, had fields of grain, greenhouses, grape arbors, and flowering gardens. His parents employed a cook, three maids, a butler, a laundress, a coachman, a chauffeur, a nurse, and a nursemaid, as well as gardeners and horse groomers.

The only child of a middle-aged father and a young mother, Franklin was the apple of both parents' eyes. Franklin's father died while he was in college, but his mother lived until Roosevelt's third term in the White House and never stopped babying him—telling him to dress warmly or put on his overshoes when it rained. Roosevelt was a happy and secure child. While few children were around for Franklin

During FDR's childhood, his Hyde Park home was surrounded by woods and fields.

to play with or study with (he was instructed at home by a tutor), Franklin spent a great deal of time sailing, hunting, and riding, as well as traveling in Europe. In fact, by the time he was 14, he had taken eight trips to Europe. When he finally did go to school, he went to good schools—to Groton (an expensive private school), to Harvard, and to Columbia Law School. Yet Roosevelt was never a highly motivated student.

Franklin's mother, Sara Delano Roosevelt, expected that Franklin would continue the tradition of overseeing the family fortunes. But when Franklin Roosevelt was in college, his fifth cousin Theodore became president of the United States. Theodore's example may well have influenced young Franklin to go into politics. When Franklin married Anna Eleanor Roosevelt, also a fifth cousin, on March 17, 1905, Theodore was a star attraction at the wedding.

The relationship between Franklin and Eleanor (or "Babs," as he called her) was unusual. Although she was his cousin and had as distinguished a family tree as he, Eleanor's childhood had been almost as unhappy as Franklin's had been serene. They had known each other since early childhood, but fell in love while Franklin was in college. Married in 1905, the couple had six children—five boys (one died in infancy) and a girl.

Their marriage was not always happy. FDR permitted his mother to dominate the family. In 1918, Franklin Roosevelt fell deeply in love with Eleanor's social secretary, Lucy Mercer. Nevertheless, his marriage to Eleanor endured, and Eleanor was there for her husband when he was struck down with polio in 1921. She had much to do with his staying in

*I*n 1895—the year before FDR left home for Groton—Charles S. Forbes painted this portrait of young Franklin. Franklin loved to ride, to hunt, and especially to sail.

Eleanor and FDR

politics. Their relationship can best be described as a magnificent working partnership.

Roosevelt entered politics at the age of 28. His first political campaign took place in 1910, when he ran for the New York State Senate. Unlike his Republican cousin Theodore, FDR ran as a Democrat. Running in a heavily Republican district—no Democrat had been elected there since 1856—Roosevelt campaigned energetically, making 10 speeches a day. He won by 1,130 votes, with a final tally of 15,708 to 14,578.

From the beginning of his career, Roosevelt was able to command the confidence of people from all walks of life. He was an early supporter of

Woodrow Wilson, who was elected president in 1912 over Theodore Roosevelt and William Howard Taft. FDR was rewarded for his support by being named assistant secretary of the navy, a position he had wanted. FDR wrote to his mother on March 17, 1913, "I am baptized, confirmed, sworn in, vaccinated—and somewhat at sea!"

FDR loved being assistant secretary of the navy. His ancestors had been whalers and merchant shippers—the sea was in his blood. He was an energetic and able administrator who put his finger into everything that concerned the navy. Roosevelt was open to new ideas, willing to take risks and be decisive. He knew how to cut through red tape and get things done, speeding up the construction of battleships and submarines.

A believer in a strong naval force, Roosevelt made an important contribution to getting the navy ready for World War I. FDR wanted very much to serve on active duty during the war, as Theodore Roosevelt had during the Spanish-American War, but he was considered too valuable to the naval department. In 1918, however, he took an official trip to Europe to talk with British naval officials on the progress of the war, to inspect American troops and naval air stations, and to rally support for the war from the Italian government. While visiting the battlefield at Verdun, Roosevelt came under enemy fire.

As assistant secretary during World War I, Roosevelt learned much about weapons manufacture, war strategy, and coordinating efforts with allies. He endeared himself to naval officers, some of whom would become the leaders of the navy during World War II. By the end of World War I, the number of ships in commission had increased more than tenfold, from 197 to 2,003.

Roosevelt's reputation as assistant secretary of the navy and his charismatic personality contributed to his nomination in 1920 as the Democratic candidate for vice president of the United States. He was only 38. He and the Democratic presidential candidate, Governor James Cox of Ohio, were badly defeated. Even so, FDR was able to build a national reputation for vigor, intelligence, and unflagging good humor.

December 1918: Aboard the USS *Aztec* in New York Harbor, FDR reviews the victorious U.S. naval fleet upon its return from Europe after World War I.

After the Republican administration of Warren Harding took over, Roosevelt returned to New York, where he made a living as a lawyer and business-person and kept his hand in politics. Six-foot-two and 175 pounds, Roosevelt was a handsome, athletic man. Then, in August 1921, while vacationing at his summer home on Campobello Island between Maine and Canada, Roosevelt contracted a severe case of polio. He never walked or stood without help again. There were many things he would never again be able to do by himself. Roosevelt's mother wanted him to retire to Hyde Park and be a country gentle-man, overseeing his investments and enjoying his many hobbies. But both his wife, Eleanor, and his friend and political advisor Louis Howe fought suc-cessfully to keep him involved in politics. They main-tained FDR's political ties while he worked on recovering the use of his legs.

Between 1922 and 1928 Roosevelt spent most of his time trying to walk again. Nevertheless, he served as floor leader at the Democratic national con-vention, directing the activities of delegates for Gover-nor Al Smith of New York, who was seeking the presidential nomination. FDR's nominating speech for Smith, whom he called the "happy warrior," was one of the highlights of the convention. Even more memorable was his slow walk to the podium to give the speech. A hushed crowd watched as Roosevelt swung himself forward toward the rostrum, first one crutch and then the other. When he reached the rostrum, Roosevelt gripped it, pushed his crutches aside, tossed his head back, and flashed his fa-mous grin.

Smith did not win the presidential nomination

FDR's early suc-cesses in politics helped prepare him for the presidency. He served as a state sen-ator for New York, as assistant secretary of the navy, and as gover-nor of New York. This election poster pictures him as a candidate for vice president in 1920. James M. Cox was the presidential nominee. The two were defeated.

in 1924, but when he did in 1928, he asked Roosevelt to run for governor of New York. After some hesitation—because he had intended to spend more time trying to regain the use of his legs—Roosevelt did run, winning by 25,564 votes. (The election was so close that Roosevelt's campaign manager, Jim Farley, did not dare go to bed for three days.)

Roosevelt proved to be an active and effective governor, continuing and expanding many of Smith's policies. Although Roosevelt did not act rapidly to deal with the Depression, he was nevertheless the first governor to set up an effective relief administration. He created jobs through state conservation projects and a system of unemployment insurance. Energetic, compassionate, and open to experiment, FDR was probably more responsive to the challenge of the Depression than any other state governor at the time. He also proved to be a phenomenal vote-getter, winning reelection in 1930 by 750,000 votes. That victory left him in an excellent position to run for the Democratic presidential nomination in 1932.

Roosevelt was considered the favorite for the 1932 Democratic presidential nomination. But he needed the votes of the delegates pledged to Speaker of the House John Nance Garner to win. After Roosevelt won these votes and became the presidential nominee, Garner became the vice-presidential nominee. FDR was heavily favored to defeat the incumbent Herbert Hoover. Roosevelt did not wage an especially impressive campaign. He avoided taking stands on important issues, such as a farm program and balancing the federal budget. In fact, he generally appeared to be a pretty ordinary politician. Nevertheless, he won with 472 electoral votes (22,800,000 popular

votes) to Hoover's 59 (15,800,000 popular votes).

In Miami, just 17 days before Roosevelt was to take office, he was the target of an assassin's bullet. A bitter 32-year-old brick mason, unemployed and ill, fired five shots at Roosevelt from a distance of 35 feet. Roosevelt was not injured, but Mayor Anton Cermak of Chicago, who was with him, was. As Roosevelt cradled Cermak in his arms, the mayor whispered, "I'm glad it was me instead of you." Cermak died on March 6. The assassin, Joseph Zangara, was convicted and executed two weeks after Roosevelt's inauguration. Roosevelt had been spared, but questions remained: What principles did he believe in? Would he be up to the challenge of leading the nation out of the Great Depression?

FDR, former presidential candidate John W. Davis (center), and Al Smith (right). When Al Smith ran for president in 1928, he encouraged FDR to run for governor of New York. Smith told FDR that being governor would not interfere with his physical therapy to recover from polio. "Don't give me that baloney," FDR replied, but he ran anyway, and won.

Although some Americans felt that FDR was a shallow "gladhander," many perceived him to be a man of substance who showed great compassion for his fellow citizens.

Roosevelt's Qualifications for the Presidency

Roosevelt seemed well qualified to be president. During his 20-year political career he had served as a state legislator and governor, been assistant secretary of the navy, and run two national campaigns. He had successfully handled major responsibilities for the navy during wartime. As governor of New York, he had dealt energetically with the Depression. He had been a very good governor of the nation's then-largest state for four years. He brought to the presidency knowledge of administration, diplomacy, politics, and the military.

Roosevelt had an enormously curious and imaginative mind that worked swiftly. He was always open to new ideas. He had a superb memory. Roosevelt was well educated and well traveled. He had a working knowledge of three foreign languages—French, Spanish, and German. He read rapidly and widely. American history particularly interested him. He also learned well by listening—a trait that would be of great assistance in the presidency.

Yet despite these qualifications, some people doubted that Roosevelt would prove to be a good president. One of the most thoughtful political commentators of the day, Walter Lippmann, said that Roosevelt was "a pleasant man who, without any important qualifications for the office, would very much like to be president." Some who remembered FDR as assistant secretary of the navy thought that he was a shallow man. They thought he lacked seriousness of purpose and the imagination to tackle a challenge as enormous as the Great Depression. They also questioned his ability to challenge powerful interest groups, like business leaders, unions, and farmers.

What many did not see in 1932 was how much Roosevelt had changed as the result of his illness. His compassion for others had grown enormously. Many couldn't see how valuable his most distinctive characteristic—boundless optimism and confidence—would be to his presidency, nor how much he would grow in office. The 91-year-old retired chief justice of the Supreme Court, Oliver Wendell Holmes, described Roosevelt well after Roosevelt paid him a visit in 1933: "A second-class intellect—but a first-class temperament."

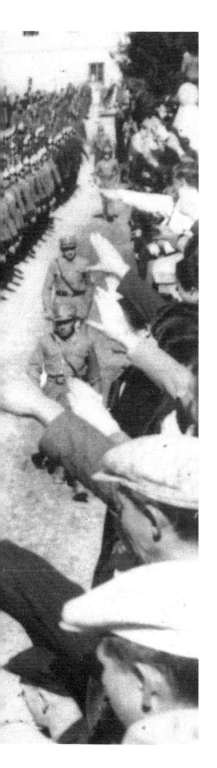

The World in 1933

*W*HEN FRANKLIN D. ROOSEVELT BEcame president, his greatest concern was getting the United States out of the Depression. Foreign affairs—the relations between the United States and other nations—were not a high priority for Roosevelt at that time.

The welfare of the rest of the world was not a high priority for Americans, either. Isolationism had been at the heart of American foreign policy for more than a hundred years, since the time of Thomas Jefferson. Americans had fought in World War I. But when that war ended in 1918 and the United States brought its troops home from Europe, Americans turned away from foreign affairs. They returned to a policy of isolation from the problems of the rest of the world.

Though Americans paid little heed, other nations

In 1938, the Nazis marched into Austria—a prelude to their annexation of much of Europe.

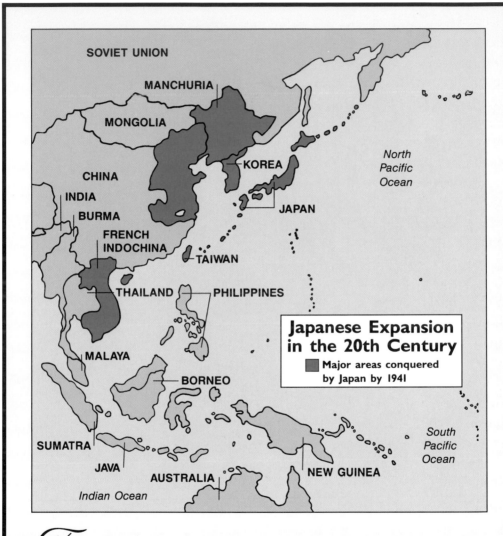

SOVIET UNION

MANCHURIA

MONGOLIA

KOREA

North
Pacific
Ocean

CHINA

INDIA

BURMA

JAPAN

FRENCH
INDOCHINA

TAIWAN

THAILAND   PHILIPPINES

**Japanese Expansion
in the 20th Century**

Major areas conquered
by Japan by 1941

MALAYA

BORNEO

SUMATRA

South
Pacific
Ocean

JAVA

AUSTRALIA   NEW GUINEA

Indian Ocean

The Japanese began to conquer other Asian nations in the early 1900s. By 1941, Japan held the shaded areas above. The threat of further Japanese expansion led the United States to declare an economic blockade against Japan in July 1941, paving the way for Japan's attack on Pearl Harbor later that year.

around the world did indeed have problems. The Great Depression of the 1930s was not limited to the United States. It affected countries in Europe too, including the Soviet Union (formerly Russia), Germany, and Italy. Unemployment soared in these countries. Rampant inflation made currency worth less than the paper it was printed on. The desperate economic straits led many citizens to frustration with their governments. That frustration paved the way for dictatorships to spring up. Perhaps even worse, the European countries controlled by dictators seemed to be ready to go to war to expand their boundaries.

The situation in Asia was also serious. The Depression of the 1930s was affecting Japan as well as the United States and Europe. A densely populated group of islands with few natural resources, Japan needed more land. The country had begun a quest for more territory early in the century, a quest that escalated in the 1930s. In 1931, Japan attacked China and swallowed up the rich province of Manchuria, establishing a puppet government there. Japan also seized nearby Formosa, Ryuku, and the Pescadores Islands. Led by Hirohito, then emperor of Japan, the Japanese also seized Korea. They took southern Sakhalin and the Kurile Islands from Russia as well.

In Russia, the Communist Party had come to power in 1917. Joseph Stalin, a cruel, paranoid dictator, was leading that country by the time of Roosevelt's inauguration in 1933. Stalin was responsible for the deaths of millions of Soviet citizens. He was willing to use force to expand the borders of his country.

Joseph Stalin ordered the death and imprisonment of millions of Soviet citizens during his rule.

The economic hardships in Europe had also paved the way for fascism to take hold in Italy. The Facist Party seized power in 1922. At the head of the party was another cruel dictator, Benito Mussolini. Mussolini eased unemployment in Italy, but at a price. His techniques for maintaining control of the government included prison camps and murder. Fascism destroyed democracy in Italy. By the time Roosevelt became president, Mussolini—who was also known as Il Duce—was readying his nation for military conquests.

Meanwhile, Germans felt frustrated and angry about the way World War I had ended in 1918. A defeated Germany had signed the Versailles Treaty. The treaty required them to make reparations, or financial compensation, to the victorious nations of

Adolf Hitler *(right)*, Germany's dictator, attended a military parade with Italy's fascist leader, Benito Mussolini *(left)*.

the war. Paying these war debts had weakened the already impoverished German economy.

The most evil and dangerous tyrant of them all was able to exploit the Germans' misery. Promising a new era of prosperity, Adolf Hitler was named chancellor of the German Republic on January 30, 1933. A few weeks later (just days after Roosevelt's inauguration), Hitler suspended parts of the German constitution—the articles guaranteeing freedom of speech, press, and assembly. Stifling all opposition, Hitler was on his way to complete power in Germany.

There were only two powerful democratic countries in Europe—Great Britain and France—to hold back the dictators. Both countries had been greatly weakened by World War I and the Great Depression. In the short run, neither would have the will

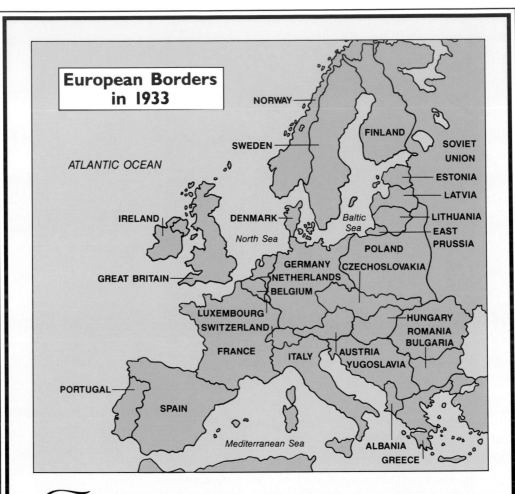

European Borders in 1933

The map above shows European borders between World War I and World War II. During that period, the German people were struggling under both an economic depression and the burden of paying reparations to the nations that had defeated them in World War I. When Hitler seized power in 1933, he was able to take advantage of his nation's frustration, winning the support of the German people as he built up the German army and prepared to invade surrounding countries.

or the leadership to meet the challenge of the aggressive dictatorships. And with the United States maintaining an isolationist policy, the French and the British couldn't expect help from the only other major democracy.

But on March 4, 1933, the potentially dangerous situation in Europe was not as significant in the minds of Americans as the crisis *within* the United States. And what a crisis it was. Virtually every part of the American economy was in disastrous shape. Of even greater concern was the fact that the American people themselves seemed to have lost confidence—in the American economy, in America's government, in the American dream.

By the time of Roosevelt's inauguration, private charities and state and local governments were already failing to do the job of providing aid to the millions of poor Americans, as President Hoover had expected they would be able to. In most states, relief payments were usually reduced to starvation level. In Detroit, for example, each person in need received only five cents per day. Not only had the Hoover administration been unsuccessful in dealing with the Depression, but President Hoover himself had been unable to communicate caring or support to the American people in their misery. Support for anti-Democratic parties and politicians on both the right and the left seemed to be growing. Would Roosevelt be up to their challenge?

Roosevelt's Beliefs

*H*OW WOULD THE NEW PRESIdent meet the challenge of the Depression? In his speech accepting the 1932 Democratic presidential nomination, Roosevelt had said:

> I pledge you, I pledge myself to a new deal for the American people. Let us all here assembled constitute ourselves prophets of a new order of competence and courage. This is more than a political campaign; it is a call to arms. Give me your help, not to win votes, but to win in this crusade to restore America to its own people.

But, crusade for what? What direction did Roosevelt want America to go? In spite of the fact that he had run for office some seven times, people were still not sure what Roosevelt stood for.

The Depression created harsh living conditions in many parts of the United States. These children lived in rural South Carolina.

*F*DR's cousin, Theodore Roosevelt, was president of the United States from 1901 to 1909. Like FDR, Teddy Roosevelt believed government should actively assist those in need.

Some of Roosevelt's beliefs, however, were indisputable. Roosevelt believed in an active, energetic government whose duty was to promote the prosperity and happiness of all Americans. He was a "progressive" in the tradition of Theodore Roosevelt and Woodrow Wilson, who believed that the government must aid the sick, the poor, and the helpless. FDR stated his philosophy in a 1931 speech:

> Modern society, acting through its government, owes the definite obligation to prevent the starvation or the due want of any of its fellow men and women who try to maintain themselves but cannot....To these unfortunate citizens, aid must be extended by Government, not as a matter of duty, but as a matter of social duty.

During the 1932 campaign, Roosevelt had made clear his support of insurance for the elderly and the unemployed. He also promised to tackle the problems of farmers. Roosevelt believed it was the federal government's responsibility to offer relief in areas where state and local aid programs could no longer help everybody in need. He supported a public works program and government regulation of agencies and people with great economic power, such as banks and stockbrokers. Roosevelt had run for president on the Democratic Party platform, which supported mortgage relief for farmers and homeowners so they would not lose their farms and homes.

Roosevelt's record as governor of New York also illustrates his beliefs. As governor, he had set up the first system of relief for unemployed people in the state's history. He provided money to prevent the needy from starving and created jobs for them on state projects. He supported aid for hard-pressed farmers and was also a strong supporter of conserving natural resources.

Of course, Roosevelt was not always consistent. In his campaign, he had said that he favored government involvement in relief and recovery, but he had also supported both a significant reduction in government spending and a balanced budget. Like almost every politician, Roosevelt tried to appeal to as many voters as possible and therefore sometimes seemed to contradict himself. On some matters, however, Roosevelt actually wanted to be inconsistent. When, for example, his campaign advisor Raymond Moley brought him two sharply conflicting statements about

---

FDR's Beliefs

*W*hen FDR became president, he believed in

- aid for the sick, poor, helpless

- insurance for the elderly and the unemployed

- mortgage relief for farmers and homeowners

- public works programs to create jobs

- regulation of banks

- conservation of natural resources

Although his own childhood was one of privilege and wealth, FDR believed that the president should stay in touch with men and women from all walks of American life.

a tariff, expecting that Roosevelt would choose one or the other, FDR instructed Moley to "weave the two together."

In the long run, Roosevelt often followed gut instincts rather than his beliefs or the particular policies he favored. This was a man who knew what it was like to be helpless, dependent on others through no fault of one's own. His compassion for those in need was enormous.

Roosevelt also believed that all problems could be solved. He had a deep confidence in the energy and inventiveness of a free society. He believed that the way to solve new and difficult problems was to experiment. As he said in one speech:

> The country needs and, unless I mistake its temper, the country demands bold persistent experimentation....The millions who are in want will not stand silently forever while the things to satisfy their needs are within easy reach.

Roosevelt was a politician, not a political philosopher. His beliefs came from many sources. He was idealistic like Woodrow Wilson and a man of action like Theodore Roosevelt. He learned a great deal from the leading social reformers of the cities, from the Columbia University professors who advised him during the 1932 campaign, and a good deal from his wife, Eleanor, a great humanitarian.

Roosevelt Makes Decisions

*P*ERHAPS THE MOST IMPORTANT rule for effective decision making by any president is to be as well informed as possible when making decisions. This is more difficult than it seems. The president is very busy, often relying on a few advisers who may only relay the messages they think the president wants to hear. Also, the longer an administration stays in power, the more it seems to disregard criticism, which it interprets as coming from political opponents.

Franklin Roosevelt usually succeeded in avoiding these problems. He compared information that came to him through "official channels" with information that came from a wide range of acquaintances. He made sure that those around him did not control his access to information. He read an enormous

FDR addressing Congress

amount: half a dozen newspapers each day, as well as countless memoranda, cables, and a sampling of mail (both pro and con).

Roosevelt was an extraordinarily accessible president. About a hundred colleagues could be put through directly to him when they called. When Congress was in session, Roosevelt spent three to four hours each day meeting with senators and representatives in person or speaking with them on the phone. Perhaps his best source of information was the stream of visitors to his office.

Roosevelt's remarkable memory gave him a superb grasp of details. He was able to retain knowledge of every department of the government, as well as considerable information about the history and geography of the United States, its politics and politicians.

Roosevelt set a standard for his administration that attracted remarkable people to government service. He brought in strong, able people, many of whom were independent enough to speak frankly to him. He chose appointees not only for their abilities and political beliefs, but for their political influence as well. His first cabinet had three Republicans and only two real New Dealers—Democrats who supported Roosevelt's legislation to combat the Depression. Former senator Cordell Hull, Roosevelt's secretary of state for three terms, was prized by the president not so much for his advice on foreign policy as for his great influence with Congress.

For most of his first two terms, Roosevelt had no large White House staff. When he took office in 1933, he had a professional staff of four: a personal secretary, an appointments secretary, a press

Cordell Hull served as secretary of state for three terms, from 1933 to 1944.

Choosing Commanders

*D*uring World War II, FDR gave Dwight D. Eisenhower *(left)* command of Operation Overlord—the D-Day invasion of Nazi-occupied France—over 366 more senior officers. Eisenhower directed the war in Europe by forging close relationships between U.S. and British commanders and by his ability to work easily with the generals who served under him.

FDR chose George Marshall *(right)* as chief of staff of the army over 34 more senior officers. Marshall greatly strengthened the U.S. Army by his choice of officers, by battling for funds, and by influencing the training of recruits. Constant, candid, and above all, honorable, he stood behind his field commanders.

secretary, and the secretary to the president. Congress added two more aides in 1936: a special counsel and a special assistant. More help was obtained by appointing persons to serve elsewhere in the government and then informally "loaning" them to the president. Nevertheless, during Roosevelt's first two terms, relatively few persons helped him directly with legislation, appointments, politics, and policy.

In 1939, Congress authorized another increase to the president's staff. Responding to a report from a committee appointed by Roosevelt, it created the Office of the President. The president was then authorized to have six administrative assistants and three secretaries.

FDR with his cabinet

These aides all reported directly to Roosevelt; he had no chief of staff. Roosevelt gave the assignments and received the work. Two aides, however, had more influence with the president than the others did—Louis Howe and Harry Hopkins, who even *lived* in the White House for a time.

One of Franklin Roosevelt's most important and trusted aides was his wife, Eleanor. Before the couple reached the White House, Eleanor had much to do with educating Franklin about the less fortunate in society and deepening his feelings for them. In the White House, she became his legs. He sent her all over the United States (and later, all over the world) to inform him about the country's problems. During Roosevelt's presidency, Eleanor traveled some

500,000 miles in the United States alone. As a powerful voice for the rights of the downtrodden, Eleanor was indispensable to her husband and his administration. She also wrote a daily newspaper column and gave countless speeches, greatly changing the nation's expectations of how the first lady should act.

One of Franklin Roosevelt's greatest strengths as a decision maker during the Depression was that he was not afraid to risk making mistakes. Another kind of president taking office in March 1933 might have appointed a commission to study what should be done about the Depression. Instead Roosevelt acted, and acted immediately. "One thing is sure," he said. "We have to do something." He would, he thought, do the best he could, and if it didn't turn out right, then he would try something else. This was the "bold, persistent experimentation" the country "demanded." Roosevelt used a baseball analogy to describe his philosophy: "I have no expectation of making a hit every time I come to bat. What I seek is the highest possible batting average."

Eleanor Roosevelt's concern for the less fortunate helped define the role of first lady as a voice for the voiceless.

Nevertheless, Roosevelt was not always as decisive as he was, for example, during the first hundred days. At times he seemed hesitant, inconsistent, and timid. Sometimes he avoided being pinned down to a policy or decision, so he could remain as flexible as possible. He knew that in a democracy, a president needs widespread support when he has to do something important. In March 1933, he had the consensus he needed because the economic situation was so bad. Later in his presidency, especially in the two years before the United States entered World War II, FDR would have to deal with a people much divided over what to do. To

BE A U.S. MARINE!
307 Evening Star Building, Washington, D. C.

FDR did not hesitate to use presidential powers to prepare the country for war.

achieve a consensus, Roosevelt sometimes encouraged those in his administration to publicly pressure him. At times, Roosevelt didn't even mind being attacked for his hesitation, as long as the effect was to educate the American people to go in the direction he really wanted to go. In other words, when Roosevelt led, he almost always was followed.

Once Roosevelt made up his mind to do something, he was not timid about finding the presidential power to do it. He was a strong leader of Congress. At the beginning of his presidency, the national emergency demanded active leadership. When the House of Representatives was considering the Emergency Banking Act, Republican floor leader Bertrand Snell said, ''The house is burning down and the President of the United States says this is the way to put out the fire.'' By the end of the first hundred days, Congress seemed to look automatically to the president for guidance. Once the emergency passed, however, Roosevelt had to bargain, barter, threaten, manipulate, and conciliate to get what he wanted from Congress.

When the country was arming for war, Roosevelt did not hesitate to use his power to seize defense plants, shipyards, and coal mines threatened by labor troubles. The plants continued normal operation, but under the watchful eyes of U.S. troops. Workers were not permitted to strike. Roosevelt created wartime agencies by executive order, funding them with money originally appropriated for other purposes. In 1942 he even told Congress that if it did not repeal a provision of the Price Control Act, he would do it himself.

As fine a president as Roosevelt was, the way he

ran the government sometimes made it difficult for others to work for him. Sometimes he gave the same task to two different persons, or made them compete for it. Often he gave more than one agency responsibility for the same job. Sometimes he chose to ignore the heads of cabinet departments and worked through their subordinates. This led to battles over "turf" between different agencies or departments and to personal battles between members of the administration. Dean Acheson, who served in several different positions in the Roosevelt administration, wrote that "what looked like chaos in the Roosevelt administration was indeed chaos."

Nevertheless, this approach to running the government had definite advantages. Roosevelt received more information, heard more than one point of view, and got feedback on how programs were working. His approach also encouraged his staff to work harder. The influence that this approach gave Roosevelt throughout his administration actually left more decisions for the president himself to make.

FDR's signature

The FDR Style

*M*OST PRESIDENTS HAVE FOUND the burdens of their office enormous, but not FDR. He loved being president. Of all the presidents, perhaps only FDR's cousin Theodore had as much fun with the presidency. In spite of the excitement and power that comes with the office, many presidents have felt lonely and agonized over the difficult decisions. Not FDR.

Perhaps Roosevelt's most striking trait as president was his confidence. Even during two of the greatest crises in American history, Roosevelt never seemed afraid—and he was able to communicate this lack of fear to the American people. Whatever the problem, Roosevelt always believed that solutions could be found and that he could help find them.

FDR's self-confidence, charisma, and obvious love for his job made him one of the most popular presidents in U.S. history.

Take these words from Roosevelt's second inaugural address:

> Many voices are heard as we face a great decision. Comfort says, "Tarry a while!" Opportunism says, "This is a good spot!" Timidity says, "How difficult is the road ahead?"
>
> If I know aught of the spirit and purpose of our Nation, we will not listen to Comfort, Opportunism, and Timidity. We will carry on.

Roosevelt was a master at communicating with the public. He practically invented the modern press conference—holding 998 conferences during the 12 years he was president. More than a hundred reporters would crowd into his office. He would have a

FDR was a master at using the press. This cartoon *(left)* shows reporters eager to hear his every word. The real press conference *(right)* shows how much he enjoyed himself.

FDR took great advantage of the media to communicate with the American people. Here he gives a radio address on the night before the 1938 congressional election.

wonderful time jesting with them and would command the headlines the next day.

Another remarkably effective way that FDR connected with the American people was by speaking over the radio. From time to time—28 times during his presidency—he gave "fireside chats." While speaking from the White House, he attempted to "see" the people to whom he was talking. He began his speeches "My Friends" and used the word "we"—making his listeners feel like they were both part of the government and the president's friends.

Roosevelt was also a splendid orator. Although sometimes as many as 25 people helped to write his speeches—including professors, poets, and playwrights—he worked on them as well. He liked to use simple, everyday language and homey illustra-

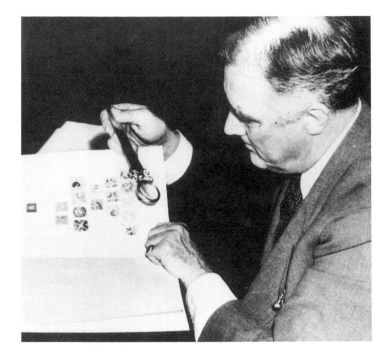

Despite the many demands of office, FDR continued to enjoy many of his hobbies—including stamp collecting—while he was president. Roosevelt even designed some stamps himself.

tions. He was a great phrasemaker, coining expressions such as "New Deal," "Good-Neighbor Policy," and "forgotten man." *Bartlett's Familiar Quotations* lists more quotations from Roosevelt than from any other president except Abraham Lincoln. Roosevelt saw the role of president as that of teacher and moral leader, and he used his press conferences, fireside chats, and speeches to that end.

What was Roosevelt really like? He had a booming laugh and a wide grin. He was rarely pompous or self-pitying and almost always charming. Roosevelt loved people and wanted them around constantly, and his White House was relaxed and informal.

He was a man of many interests. He collected a number of things—ship models and books about the navy, but most of all, stamps. His stamp collection

The Stirring Words of FDR

This generation of Americans has a rendezvous with destiny.

In the field of world policy, I would dedicate this nation to the policy of the good neighbor.

We are now in this war. We are all in it all the way. Every single man, woman, and child is a partner in the most tremendous undertaking of our American history. We must share together the bad news and the good news, the defeats and the victories—the changing fortunes of war.

Freedom of conscience, of education, of speech, of assembly are among the very fundamentals of democracy and all of them would be nullified should freedom of the press ever be successfully challenged.

The test of our progress is not whether we add more to the abundance of those who have much; it is whether we provide enough for those who have too little.

contained 1,250,000 stamps! He loved to draw and design things, from bookplates to aircraft carriers to a square coin. Most of all, he loved sailing and the sea.

But Roosevelt was a very, very private man. He shared his deepest hopes and fears with nobody—not even his wife. He never shared his feelings about his terrible illness with anyone. Roosevelt hid his deepest emotions from the world by wearing masks of warmth and courtesy. He cheered and inspired everyone around him, but he did not confide his feelings to them.

It is incredible to realize that this man, who carried the hopes and fears of the nation during the Great Depression and World War II, could not walk or stand without help and had to be lifted in and out of beds, cars, and wheelchairs. He had to be bathed, dried, and dressed by someone else. But Roosevelt never appeared helpless or dependent in public, and he rarely failed to smile in public or in private. His illness must have increased his compassion for others. He admitted that it taught him patience. In one of the few remarks he made to anyone about his illness, he said, "If you had spent two years in bed trying to wiggle your big toe, after that anything else would seem easy."

FDR's own physical limitations contributed to his great compassion for the downtrodden.

Putting an End to Fear: the First Hundred Days

*A*S HE BEGAN HIS FIRST TERM, Franklin Roosevelt had two immediate, urgent tasks. The first was to deal with the banking crisis. The second was to restore the American people's faith in America itself. He achieved both within 10 days and kept right on going.

He began, of course, with that magnificent inaugural address calling for sacrifice, discipline, and action. On his first night in office he did not attend the inaugural ball, but instead spent the time conferring with Louis Howe, his political mentor. The next day—a Sunday—FDR issued a proclamation calling Congress into special session the following

Police officers had to control crowds after the Wall Street panic of October 1929.

FDR's first of many fireside chats served to reassure Americans during the banking crisis.

Thursday. Hours later he issued another proclamation closing all banks in the United States until the following Friday and prohibiting the export of gold and silver. On Monday he explained the proclamation to reporters and gave a short speech over the radio calling for sacrifice and devotion to country. The national mood had begun to change already.

The special session of Congress came to be known as the Hundred Days. By the time the session opened, the Roosevelt administration had two bills ready. One was an emergency banking bill. The other bill called for sharp cuts in government spending to restore the confidence of bankers and big business in the government. Before the session began, Roosevelt had already explained the banking bill to leaders of Congress and held his first informal press conference.

Never in American history had Congress responded so rapidly to a presidential request. The House of Representatives began its debate on the emergency banking bill on March 9, 1933, at 2:55 in the afternoon, even before it received printed copies of the bill. No one spoke against the bill, and it passed in little more than an hour. In the Senate, the bill met some opposition, but it still passed before the end of the day, by a vote of 73 to 7. The president signed the bill into law before 9:00 on the evening of the day the bill had been introduced.

The Emergency Banking Act authorized government assistance to private banks so that they could reopen. It provided for an orderly system to reopen sound banks and keep insolvent ones closed.

On Friday the president sent his second message to Congress, asking it to adopt the Economy Bill to cut government spending by half a billion dollars.

FDR's First Fireside Chat on Banking

*I*n the first of his famous fireside chats, FDR encouraged Americans to trust the banks again. He said:

Confidence and courage are the essentials of success in carrying out our plan. You people must have faith; you must not be stampeded by rumors or guesses. Let us unite in banishing fear. We have provided the machinery to restore our financial system; it is up to you to support and make it work.

It is your problem no less than it is mine. Together we cannot fail.

Even though the bill cut veterans' benefits (a very unpopular action) and the pay of government employees, it was passed by both houses of Congress the next day.

On Sunday, March 12, Roosevelt spoke to the nation over the radio. In this, the first of his fireside chats, Roosevelt told 60 million listeners that it was now safe to use the banks. "I can assure you," he said, "that it is safer to keep your money in a reopened bank than under the mattress."

The next day the banks reopened in many cities. Far more people deposited than withdrew money. In little more than a week, the nation had regained confidence in both the government and itself. The reaction of the American people to Roosevelt was remarkable. Within the first few days following the inauguration, 500,000 Americans wrote to the White House to express their appreciation.

The Civilian Conservation Corps (CCC) gave 2.5 million out-of-work Americans jobs. This CCC worker digs in a quarry.

Roosevelt took advantage of the momentum of the nation's changing mood. He sent a whirlwind of proclamations, executive orders, and messages to Congress. Under his direction, a host of advisors drafted and redrafted bills. Changing his original plan, the president kept Congress in session after it passed the banking and economy bills. By the time Congress adjourned on June 16, it had approved 15 major laws. Brilliantly led by the president's bargaining, bartering, and wheedling, Congress passed laws to aid national recovery, to reform the economy, and to relieve the human pain of the Depression. No Congress has ever responded so rapidly to a president's proposals. For a little more than three months, Roosevelt helped to keep the national mood confident by never giving Americans time to lose hope. Much of the New Deal was created during these first hundred days.

Laws such as the Agricultural Adjustment Act restored farmers' incomes by limiting the growth of certain crops that had been overloading the market. The Emergency Farm Mortgage Act provided a way to save farms from foreclosure. Other laws created jobs. Over the course of 10 years, the Civilian Conservation Corps provided outdoor jobs for 2.5 million young people: planting trees, building roads, and improving national parks. The Public Works Administration created jobs with major building projects such as the Grand Coulee Dam, New York's Triborough Bridge, and Chicago's sewage system. The National Industrial Recovery Act not only provided jobs but also attempted to improve wages and working conditions and to end wasteful competition. Two more new laws regulated the banking system. The Securities Act intended to protect stock buyers from fraud, while another law created a system to insure depositors in the event of bank failure.

The Tennessee Valley Authority (TVA) was created to build a chain of dams on the Tennessee River (which winds through seven states). The dams would help control floods and protect forests while producing cheap water power for electricity. The Federal Emergency Relief Act authorized half a billion

FDR visited the Grand Coulee Dam in October 1937. The dam was one of many public works programs sponsored by the New Deal.

Presidential Powers

*F*DR's forceful use of presidential powers during genunine national emergencies set a precedent that would be abused by later presidents, especially by Lyndon Johnson and Richard Nixon.

In 1964, Congress approved the Gulf of Tonkin Resolution, which gave President Johnson the power to take "all necessary measures to repel any armed attack against the forces of the United States and to prevent further aggression." As the Vietnam War dragged on, many Americans became critical of Johnson's use of these powers to send so many American troops overseas.

In 1973, President Nixon was forced to reveal that he had been making secret tapes of conversations in the White House since 1971. When asked to turn the tapes over to a Senate investigative committee, Nixon refused, saying that the Constitution gave him the right to maintain the secrecy of the tapes if their exposure could endanger the presidency. It was Nixon's belief that as president, he was above the law. This attitude contributed to the Watergate scandal that led to his resignation.

dollars for the relief of people left in desperate straits by the Depression.

Roosevelt's New Deal turned out to be a series of measures, many experimental, that tried to provide the "three R's" the nation needed—relief, recovery, and reform. Relief programs saved millions from hunger. Programs that created jobs poured millions of dollars into the economy, bringing about a crucial short-run recovery. Important reforms affected virtually every area of the economy.

Some of FDR's critics compared him to Hitler and Stalin because the programs of his New Deal greatly increased the power and size of the national government. In spite of this attack and other bitter accusations that the New Deal was "socialistic" or "communistic," it was not as radical as many of its opponents claimed. Roosevelt had a very deep faith in democracy and the common people. "My anchor is democracy—and more democracy," he said. While the New Deal did increase the size and activities of the federal government, and the president and the executive branch did gain in power compared to Congress, the accomplishments of the Roosevelt administration promoted democracy, kept capitalism alive, and restored faith in the constitutional government.

Nevertheless, the New Deal did not fully lick the Great Depression. As late as 1939, 17 percent of America's workers were still unemployed.

Fighting for Social Security

*F*RANKLIN DELANO ROOSEVELT
was no revolutionary—although he was
sometimes accused of being one. He took the
capitalist system for granted. He believed, however,
that changes were needed to make the system fairer
and more humane so that all would share in its plenty.

In the spring of 1935, Franklin Delano Roosevelt
decided to fight for passage of a law creating the
social security system. This decision greatly affected
(and continues to affect) the lives of tens of millions
of Americans. The social security law created a system to provide help for those who are fired and
looking for work, welfare for those in dire need,
and pensions (regular payments) to retired older
Americans. By passing the law, Congress made clear
that the federal government (along with state governments) has a responsibility to provide the American

FDR fought for the social security system—a system designed
to protect and provide aid for millions of unemployed and retired
Americans.

people with some protection from the difficulties of life.

FDR strongly believed that one of the things government should do was try to make life easier for its citizens. To a reporter's question about the social objective of his administration, Roosevelt answered:

> The social objective, I should say, remains just what it was, which is to do what any honest Government of any country would do: try to increase the security and the happiness of a larger number of people in all occupations of life and in all parts of the country, to give them more of the good things of life, to give them a greater distribution not only of wealth in the narrow terms, but of wealth in the wider terms; to give them places to go in the summertime—recreation; to give them assurance that they are not going to starve in their old age; to give honest business a chance to go ahead and make a reasonable profit; and to give everyone a chance to earn a living.

At the time Roosevelt became president, some governments of European nations had already begun insuring their citizens against various catastrophic events that make it impossible to earn a living— physical disability, old age, the closing of a factory. Germany had been the first in the 1880s. England and France followed in the early years of the twentieth century. When Roosevelt became president, however, Wisconsin was the only one of the 48 states to have a similar system. Franklin Roosevelt was the first leading U.S. politician to support national unemployment insurance. He first voiced this support in a speech to the National Governor's Conference on June 30, 1930.

Destitute and homeless, some New York City residents lived in shacks in Central Park during the winter of 1932–33.

In spite of support for such a system, Roosevelt did not include it in his agenda for the Hundred Days. In fact, he did not begin to get around to it until late in the spring of 1934, when it already had considerable backing in Congress. On June 8, 1934, Roosevelt sent a message to Congress supporting a system of social insurance. Roosevelt said the system had to involve both the national government and the states, be financially sound, and be paid for by the contributions of both workers and their employers.

Several weeks later, Roosevelt named a Committee on Economic Security to develop a system of social insurance for those too old or ill or disabled to work, and for those laid off by their employers. The committee was made up of five members of Roosevelt's cabinet and was chaired by Secretary of Labor Frances Perkins, the first woman ever to serve in the cabinet.

The committee did not report until January 15, 1935. By that time, Roosevelt's "Big Mo," that is, the momentum of the Hundred Days, had run out. In 1934, FDR had suffered a number of defeats

FDR with his cabinet in 1933

in Congress on important issues. Although the Democratic Party had won a tremendous victory in the 1934 congressional elections, in 1935 Roosevelt did not seem to be giving the country a sense of direction. Attempting to please a variety of groups, he came under increasing attack. The business community criticized Roosevelt for too much government involvement in the economy. Labor leaders and liberals attacked Roosevelt for not doing more to relieve the Depression and reform the economy.

This issue was a good example of Roosevelt's uncertainty. Although he had committed himself to social security in the spring of 1934, by November he seemed to be backing away from fighting for old-age security because it did not look as if he could win. Yet in his State of the Union Address early in 1935, Roosevelt said that he would shortly send a bill to Congress covering both unemployment and old-age benefits, as well as benefits for children, mothers, and the handicapped. Then, two days after the Committee on Economic Security gave him its report (January 15, 1935), he did send a message to Congress calling for a national system providing wage earners income upon retirement (if they did not live to retirement, their survivors would receive the income) and for a system of unemployment compensation on a state-by-state basis. Having sent the message to Congress, however, Roosevelt did not appear to be willing to fight hard for it.

The social security bill and other important bills seemed to be gathering dust in Congress early in 1935. Not until May did the president really begin to press. Then, suddenly, Roosevelt began to insist on passage of five major pieces of legislation, including social

Secretary of Labor Frances Perkins was the first woman to serve in a presidential cabinet.

All U.S. citizens are entitled to a social security number.

security. The result was what has been called the "Second Hundred Days" (or the "Second New Deal").

Roosevelt asked for passage of a law greatly changing labor-management relations, a "soak-the-rich" tax bill, a law governing holding companies in the public utility area, a banking bill, and the Social Security Act. Why did he wait so long to offer this strong leadership—especially regarding social security? It is hard to be sure. He may have had some doubts about the details of the proposals themselves. Some say that he waited until he was sure the bill was going to pass and then stepped in to get some of the credit. More likely, Roosevelt was worried that his support of the social security bill and some of the other bills would seriously decrease his popularity with the business community. Until the spring of 1935, he had tried to aid the "common people"—the farmers, the laborers, the very poor—while trying to gain and keep the support of the leaders of "big business." In the spring of 1935, Roosevelt may have concluded that keeping the support of both would not be possible and he had to choose sides. Soon, he would be hammering away at his enemies in the corporate world, calling them "economic royalists."

Some of the opposition seems hard to believe. The bill was not only attacked for its cost but also for violating the values of thrift and self-help. Conservative opponents argued that with unemployment insurance, nobody would work, and with old-age survivors' insurance, nobody would save. For example, Senator A. Henry Moore of New Jersey argued against the bill, saying:

> It would take all the romance out of life. We might as well take a child from the nursery, give him a nurse, and protect him from every experience that life affords.

The opponents of the bill even called it slavery, arguing that it would lead to national bankruptcy, moral decay, and the collapse of the republic.

Nevertheless, once Roosevelt got into the fight, the social security bill moved rapidly through Congress. When he signed the bill into law on August 14, 1935, the president said, "Today a hope of many years' standing is in large part fulfilled." He added:

> If the Senate and the House of Representatives in this long and arduous session had done nothing more than pass this bill, the session would be regarded as historic for all time.

The major purpose of the Social Security Act was, as Roosevelt wrote, "to provide the average worker with some assistance that when cycles of unemployment come or when his working days are over, he will have enough money to live decently."

Two jobless men read want ads on a Washington, D.C., park bench.

The new law provided that at age 65, workers would receive a pension, the size of which would relate to what they had earned. All workers would have their paychecks individually taxed for social security. Employers would pay a payroll tax. The federal government would also share with the states the care of those very poor people over 65 who would not be able to take part in the old-age system. The law also provided that the federal government would join with each state in a system of unemployment compensation to tide workers over between jobs. The federal government would also cooperate with the states to help dependent mothers and children, the crippled, and the blind.

The law was far from perfect. It did not, for example, cover farm laborers and domestic servants, and it did not cover those who lost their jobs because of illness. Regardless of its weaknesses, the law that passed in 1935 became what Roosevelt said it would become—a foundation that would provide "a real form of financial security for workers." Never before had the United States government touched so many lives. Nearly 60 years later, social security has become an almost untouchable part of American life.

Each of the laws Roosevelt strongly supported in May 1935 passed, although not all became law in exactly the same way he had hoped. By the end of this session, Congress had accomplished almost as much as it had during the first hundred days. The work of the Second New Deal, especially the Social Security Act, clinched for Roosevelt such overwhelming support that when he ran for reelection in 1936, he won 46 of 48 states.

Packing the Supreme Court

*P*ROBABLY FDR'S WORST DECISION
as president occurred in 1937. He decided
to ask Congress to pass a law increasing the
number of justices on the Supreme Court from
9 to 15. He believed that the Court was blocking
the nation's economic recovery. This decision led
to one of the biggest political battles of the twentieth century.

Many of the important laws passed in the early
years of the New Deal greatly increased the powers
of the federal government. Some of the laws raised
difficult constitutional questions. Did Congress have
the power to regulate the number of hours a miner
could work? Could legislation force corporations to
deal with labor unions? Could the Congress pay
farmers not to grow wheat? Roosevelt believed that
there was ample power in the Constitution to deal

Chief Justice Charles Evans Hughes *(standing at podium)* addressed
Congress on its 150th anniversary.

with an emergency like the Great Depression. As he said in his first inaugural address:

> Our Constitution is so simple and practical that it is possible always to meet extraordinary needs by changes in emphasis and arrangement without loss of essential form.

Others felt differently, however. Some leaders of corporations and banks objected to the expensive relief programs of the New Deal, the support for labor, and the growth of the federal government.

During the first two years of Roosevelt's presidency, it looked like the Supreme Court would uphold the major laws of the New Deal, although by

The 1936 Supreme Court. FDR believed the decisions of this court were blocking the nation's recovery.

uncomfortably close votes. In 1935 and 1936, however, the Supreme Court struck down a number of important laws passed by Congress (and state legislatures) dealing with the Depression. Twelve laws passed by Congress—including laws dealing with farming, railroads, and the coal industry—were ruled unconstitutional. Roosevelt was upset enough by these decisions to declare at a press conference that the Court had put the country back in the "horse-and-buggy" age. His concern about the Supreme Court grew, as other important New Deal laws such as the National Labor Relations Act and the Social Security Act made their way up to the Court.

Roosevelt waited until a few weeks after the 1936 election to do something about the Court. That election had given the Democrats overwhelming control of the Senate (76 out of 96 votes) and of the House of Representatives (331 out of 433 votes).

Roosevelt might have tried to do a number of things in dealing with the Supreme Court. He could have done nothing at all and simply waited. Sooner or later, several of the justices would retire or die, and Roosevelt could appoint their successors. Five of the justices were over 75 years old and a sixth over 70. But it may have seemed to Roosevelt that the four most conservative justices of the Court—all of whom were over 70—were trying to outlast him. Not a single justice left the Court during his first term.

Roosevelt could also have proposed an amendment to the Constitution that would have made it unmistakably clear that the federal government had the power to deal with the Depression. While it takes a two-thirds vote from each house of the Congress and three-quarters of the state legislatures to amend the Constitution, Roosevelt might well have succeeded if he had tried this approach. But, he could not be entirely sure that he would succeed, and it often takes a good deal of time to amend the Constitution.

Instead, Roosevelt tried to have Congress pass a law allowing him to appoint one new justice for each sitting justice who was over the age of 70. This would have immediately given him six appointments to the Court—and a safe majority. Congress already had the power to change the size of the Supreme Court, and it had in fact done so at other times in American history, although never in the drastic manner that Roosevelt proposed. Unlike a constitutional amendment, a bill to increase the size of the Supreme Court needed only a majority of those voting in the Congress in order to pass.

Roosevelt's remarkable political gifts—his ability to stay in touch with public opinion, his timing, his sense of when to compromise—deserted him during the court-packing battle. The decision to "pack" the Supreme Court was made differently from almost every other important decision of his presidency. FDR talked the matter over with only one advisor—Attorney General Homer Cummings. FDR didn't speak with others in his cabinet or consult a single member of Congress. Nor did he talk with the leaders of groups that were among his strongest supporters—unions, farmers, and liberals. He didn't even float any "trial balloons"—informal proposals designed to measure public support. Instead, he went out on a limb—all by himself. As a result, he was unprepared for the enormous opposition his proposal received. Republicans and

The Supreme Court building. FDR discovered that the Supreme Court was a sturdy institution he could not easily change.

Democrats, liberals and conservatives, northerners and southerners alike opposed this bill. Many thought that the Constitution itself was threatened by it. Then, as the battle raged, Roosevelt never showed his characteristic flexibility and therefore missed opportunities for compromise that might have permitted him to name a couple of justices almost immediately.

The first mistake Roosevelt made in the court-packing fight was underestimating the amount of opposition to his plan. The second mistake was the way he explained the decision to the nation. Instead of finding a straightforward way to tell the American

Chief Justice Hughes op-
posed FDR's plan to in-
crease the number of
Supreme Court justices.

people why he felt such a law was necessary, he first
told them that his proposal was needed because the
justices were too old to work efficiently:

> Even at the present time the Supreme Court is labor-
> ing under a heavy burden....A part of the problem
> of obtaining a sufficient number of judges to dispose
> of cases is the capacity of the judges themselves.
> This brings forward the question of aged or infirm
> judges—a subject of delicacy and yet one which re-
> quires frank discussion.

But in a letter to the Senate Judiciary Committee, Chief Justice Charles Evans Hughes pointed
out that FDR's judgment was wrong. Hughes
demonstrated that the Court was "fully abreast of
its work." In addition, he argued that an increase
in the number of Supreme Court justices would harm
the Court's efficiency. He wrote, "There would
be more judges to hear, more judges to confer,
more judges to discuss, more judges to convince
and to decide."

FDR did not reveal to the nation the real reason
for his proposal until a month after he announced
his court-packing plan:

> I want to talk with you simply about the need for
> present action in this crisis—the need to meet the
> unanswered challenge of one-third of a nation ill-
> nourished, ill-clad, ill-housed.

Roosevelt said that whenever the Congress had
tried to help farmers, improve conditions for workers,
protect businesses from unfair competition, and con-
serve natural resources, the Court had ruled the laws
unconstitutional. But FDR suspected the Court did

not really believe the laws were unconstitutional, only unwise. He went on:

> [We] have therefore, reached a point as a nation where we must take action to save the Constitution from the Court and the Court from itself. We must find a way to take an appeal from the Supreme Court and to the Constitution itself.

By not being candid from the beginning, however, Roosevelt had hurt his cause. The president lost his struggle to pack the Court after a tremendous battle.

Four events in particular doomed the court-packing proposal. The first was the letter by Chief Justice Hughes.

The second blow to Roosevelt's plan came on March 29, 1937, as the Court handed down the first of a series of decisions holding important New Deal and state laws constitutional. The most important of these was the decision to uphold the National Labor Relations Act and the decision to uphold the Social Security Act. Within two months, the Court upheld two of the most important New Deal laws. Suddenly it seemed unlikely that the Court would strike down other federal and state laws dealing with the economy. While these decisions supported FDR's plan for national recovery, they greatly weakened his argument that the Court was anti-New Deal.

The third blow came on May 18, with Justice Willis Van Devanter's carefully timed announcement of his retirement. Van Devanter was one of the most conservative members of the Court. His retirement gave Roosevelt an immediate opportunity to appoint a liberal justice—again weakening his stand against the Court.

FDR's court-packing plan did not contribute to his popularity, as this cartoon illustrates.

The final blow came with the unexpected death of the Senate majority leader, Joseph Robinson of Arkansas, who had been the most powerful supporter of the court-packing bill in the Senate.

Had Roosevelt been willing to compromise a bit earlier, he probably could have gotten a bill through Congress that would have permitted him a total of three appointments (including that to replace Van Devanter) in less than a year. On July 22, however, a little more than a week after Robinson's death, the Senate killed the bill.

The defeat was not politically fatal for Roosevelt, but never again would the Congress (even with the huge Democratic majority) act as a "rubber stamp" for him. The Supreme Court survived its greatest threat in American history. Yet the Court also had to make way for progress. In less than 10 years, the Court overturned almost every constitutional principle that could have been used to reject liberal legislation, thus dramatically modernizing the Constitution. The Court upheld the law setting a national minimum wage and a maximum work week. It also upheld the Second Agricultural Adjustment Act regulating farmers, the law giving the federal government the power to tax the employees of state governments, and the wartime regulation of rents.

In the remaining years of FDR's presidency, the death and retirement of seven justices permitted Roosevelt to appoint replacements. Among his appointees were some of the most able men any president has ever appointed to the Supreme Court: Hugo Black, Felix Frankfurter, Robert Jackson, and Wiley Rutledge, to name four. The Court made up of Franklin Roosevelt's appointees did more to protect civil liberties than the Supreme Court had ever done before in American history.

In the end, Roosevelt both lost and won. Not only did Congress reject the court-packing plan, but the wounds from the battle among Democrats in the Congress never completely healed. Never again would Roosevelt be as effective in dealing with the Congress as he had been before the court-packing fight. Yet Roosevelt also achieved a victory: during the struggle, the Supreme Court changed some important views about the Constitution. The Court would never again hold a New Deal law unconstitutional.

Trading Destroyers for Bases

*L*ATE IN THE SUMMER OF 1940, Franklin Roosevelt made one of the most important decisions ever made by a president of the United States. He chose to help Great Britain in a time of desperate peril—bringing the United States closer to involvement in World War II. Roosevelt decided to send Britain 50 old (but still usable) destroyers, in return for 99-year leases on eight military bases in the western hemisphere.

Franklin Roosevelt had always believed that the United States should play an active, important role in world affairs. When he became president, however, the American people were still committed to isolationism—the policy of staying out of Europe's problems. To maintain this policy, Congress passed

On December 7, 1941, Japanese war planes attacked the U.S. fleet at Pearl Harbor, drawing the United States into World War II.

Neutrality Acts in 1935 and 1936. In the event of war, these acts required the president to proclaim an arms embargo (prohibit the sale of arms and ammunition) both against the nation or nations that started the war and also against the country or countries under attack. Congress had also barred loans to any country at war and banned the use of American ships for trade with any country at war. Roosevelt opposed the Neutrality Acts because he wanted the United States to give up isolationism—but because the Neutrality Acts regulated arms traffic (and because of political pressure), he signed them into law.

FDR had not made much of an effort during his first term to involve the nation in European affairs. He was more concerned with fighting the Depression at home. He was also aware that some of the strongest supporters of the New Deal in Congress were isolationists, and realized that a large majority of the American people supported isolationism. FDR did not act forcefully when Italy invaded Ethiopia in 1935. Nor did he act when Hitler openly re-armed Germany that same year and sent troops to the Rhineland region of Germany in 1936, even though both of Hitler's actions violated the Versailles Treaty.

Before World War II broke out, Roosevelt's major attempt to educate the American people about the growing dangers in the world had been in a speech he gave in Chicago on October 5, 1937. In that speech, he said that nations who make wars of aggression ought to be isolated by other nations. He suggested this isolation be enforced by statements condemning them, by breaking diplomatic relations, but possibly also by cutting off trade.

> When an epidemic of physical disease starts to spread, the community approves and joins in a quarantine of the patients in order to protect the health of the community against the spread of the disease.

Roosevelt's speech received mixed reactions. He encountered sharp criticism from isolationist leaders and the isolationist press. Yet mail to the president was favorable, as were most newspaper editorials. But the American people were not yet ready for involvement in European affairs.

Roosevelt was successful in building up the U.S. armed forces before war broke out in Europe. One

In violation of the Versailles Treaty, Hitler *(standing in car)* began to rearm Germany in 1935, in preparation for the invasion of much of Europe.

This cartoon from the 1930s shows the reluctance of Americans to get involved in problems outside of their own country.

of the New Deal's early programs to create jobs had involved the construction of naval vessels. In 1938 Hitler seized the Sudetenland region of Czechoslovakia—indicating his willingness to go to the brink of war, as well as Britain's and France's unwillingness to stop him. In response, Roosevelt announced plans for a tremendous expansion of the air force.

The first stage of World War II began in September 1939, when Germany and the Soviet

Union attacked Poland. Great Britain and France came to Poland's defense by declaring war on Germany. Most Americans wanted Great Britain and France to win, but virtually all Americans wanted the United States to stay out of the war.

Roosevelt believed that once Hitler had conquered Europe, he would go after the United States. Limited by the Neutrality Acts and aware of U.S. support for isolationism, the president acted slowly but decisively.

He readied the armed forces, cautiously tried to help Great Britain, and tried to educate the American people through speeches, press conferences, and fireside chats. Sometimes he backtracked and reassured the public before educating them some more. Often he let others take the lead and waited for public opinion to catch up. Gradually, very gradually, the American people came to believe that the risk of involvement in the war was less than was the risk of British defeat. The president nudged the United States ever closer to active involvement in the war against Hitler. But Roosevelt was not always truthful in the process. He made some promises he knew he couldn't keep, and sometimes he made important decisions without consulting the Congress. Nevertheless, Roosevelt's basic judgment was correct—Hitler would have proved to be an even greater danger to the United States had he conquered Britain.

Immediately after the war began in Europe, Roosevelt proclaimed American neutrality. He also said, however, that while "this nation must remain a neutral nation," he could not "ask that every American remain neutral in thought as well." Roosevelt was successful in convincing Congress to repeal the law that prohibited the sale of arms to nations at war, so long as the buyer paid cash and took the responsibility of shipping the arms. Nevertheless, early in 1940, only 23 percent of Americans polled believed that the United States should become involved in the European war even if France and Britain were defeated.

Germany and the Soviet Union took only one month to overrun Poland. During the following winter, nothing much seemed to happen. But on April 9, 1940, Hitler launched a series of attacks, and—with terrifying suddenness—overran first Denmark and Norway, then Belgium, Holland, and Luxembourg. By the middle of June, France had surrendered. These events stunned the American people and, for the first time, brought home to many of them the nature of the threat to the United States.

Nevertheless, American opinions remained divided. Opposition to intervention on behalf of Great Britain was particularly strong in the Midwest and West, among American citizens of German, Italian, and Irish background, as well as pacifists and radicals. Intervention did have considerable support, however, among liberal Democrats and conservative Republicans in both the Northeast and the South.

By this time Roosevelt had come to believe that American involvement in the European war was inevitable. After Hitler's invasions in May 1940, Roosevelt called for the building of 50,000 airplanes and an appropriation of $896 million for national defense.

Roosevelt now had some leeway to aid Great Britain, if he did so cautiously. British pilots were allowed to train in Florida. Damaged British warships could be repaired in American shipyards. Roosevelt gave a number of older planes to airplane manufacturers, with the understanding that as the manufacturers built newer models of airplanes, the older ones would be transferred to Great Britain.

But this was not enough. A German invasion across the English Channel was being readied. By the summer of 1940, Britain had lost nearly half of its destroyer force for the defense of the channel and

German soldiers drive through a destroyed Polish city in 1939.

Nazi Germany began to invade neighboring countries in 1939 and launched an attack against Great Britain in 1940. By the summer of 1941, the Nazis had overtaken most of Europe. Not until the United States entered World War II in December 1941 did the European Allies feel that they could defeat Hitler.

was under constant bombardment by the German air force. By August, about 1,500 Nazi aircraft were attacking every day. Winston Churchill, prime minister of Great Britain, rallied his people for their "finest hour." But he needed help from the United States, and he turned to Roosevelt.

Churchill had already asked the United States for 50 "overage" (surplus) destroyers to help fight the invasion. Under U.S. law, Roosevelt could only send destroyers to Britain if the navy stated that they were "useless." Naval officials, however, had recently told Congress that the vessels were still usable. Roosevelt could have sought congressional approval, but Congress was already occupied with a bitter debate over

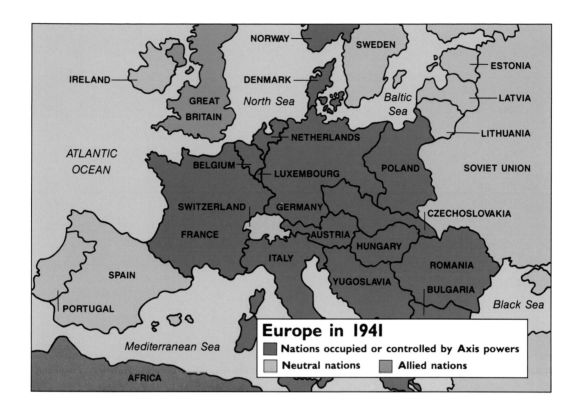

Europe in 1941

- ■ Nations occupied or controlled by Axis powers
- ☐ Neutral nations   ■ Allied nations

whether or not to create a military draft. Thus, there might have been a long delay before Congress acted or, worse yet, Congress might have turned the president down.

Roosevelt wanted to send the destroyers to Great Britain, but he didn't want to break the law or violate the Constitution. He also didn't want to give the Republicans an election issue. He looked for a legitimate way to act with the support of public opinion.

At a cabinet meeting on August 2, three "hawks" (supporters of greater involvement in the war) suggested that the United States trade its old destroyers for 99-year leases on British military bases in the

British sailors load their duffel bags onto one of the overage destroyers headed to Great Britain in 1940.

western hemisphere. This way, Roosevelt could not be accused of "giving away" American property and might even be praised for driving a sharp bargain. By late August, millions of signatures had been gathered by a citizens' committee on a petition urging the president to act.

On September 3, as the Battle for Britain reached its height, Roosevelt used his authority as commander in chief to trade the 50 still usable destroyers for leases on six bases in the western hemisphere. At the same time, Great Britain "gave" the United States sites for two more bases—in Newfoundland and Bermuda. When Roosevelt reported to Congress, he called the trade the "most important action in the reinforcement of our national defense that has been taken since the Louisiana Purchase.'' The deal would prevent the bases from falling into German hands and permit the United States to defend itself well out into the Atlantic. But the true significance of the deal was that it brought the United States that much closer to open support of Great Britain.

Great Britain withstood heavy bombing in the summer and fall of 1940, but continued to be in peril. Hitler's invasion had been avoided—but perhaps only temporarily. After Roosevelt won a third term as president in November 1940, Churchill made another urgent request for arms and food. This time, though, Churchill said that Britain could no longer afford to pay for the aid. The United States had lent money to European allies during World War I and had never been paid back by any nation other than Finland— something the American people greatly resented. Loaning Britain money for food and arms seemed politically impossible.

Roosevelt came up with lend-lease, a simple solution that he sold to the country magnificently. The United States would send Britain the arms it needed immediately and without charge. Once the war ended, the original goods would either be returned, or the United States would be repaid in kind. Roosevelt used a marvelous illustration to let the country in on the idea at a press conference in December 1940:

> Suppose my neighbor's house catches on fire, and I have a length of garden hose four or five hundred feet away. If he can take my garden hose and connect it up with his hydrant, I may help him to put out his fire. Now what do I do? I don't say to him before that operation, ''Neighbor, my garden hose

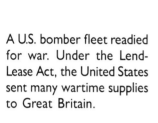

A U.S. bomber fleet readied for war. Under the Lend-Lease Act, the United States sent many wartime supplies to Great Britain.

cost me $15; you have to pay me for it." What is the transaction that goes on? I don't want $15— I want my garden hose back after the fire is over. All right, if it goes through the fire all right, intact, without any damage to it, he gives it back to me and thanks me very much for the use of it.

But if the hose is ruined, the neighbor could simply replace it.

Roosevelt followed this up with a fireside chat to once again explain to the American people the danger they were in and the role America should play.

There is far less chance of the United States getting into war if we do all we can now to support the nations defending themselves against attack by the Axis [Germany, Italy, and Japan] than if we acquiesce in their defeat, submit tamely to an Axis victory, and wait our turn to be the object of attack in another war later on.

What could Americans do? What should they do? They should produce weapons to aid the fight against Hitler. "We must be the great arsenal of democracy," the president declared.

Lend-lease passed the House of Representatives 260-165 in February 1941 and the Senate 60-31 in March. When Roosevelt signed the bill into law on March 15, he used the occasion to try once again to influence American opinion. He also tried to lift British spirits.

> The British people...need ships. From America, they will get ships. They need planes. From America, they will get planes. Yes, from America they need food, and from America they will get food.

Adolf Hitler in 1933, the year he became chancellor of Germany

Five minutes after signing the lend-lease law, Roosevelt approved a list of items for immediate shipment to Great Britain. While the debate in Congress had been going on, the president had worked up the list. The very next day he asked Congress for an immediate appropriation of seven billion dollars to pay for the act. Congress passed such a bill less than two weeks later.

Lend-lease was not the act of a neutral power. Under international law, Germany would have been within its rights to declare war upon the United States. But Hitler did not want a war with the United States at that particular time, so he ignored the provocation.

Other non-neutral acts by the United States followed. U.S. patrols protected British ships carrying armaments and food in the Atlantic. The United States occupied Greenland, a possession of Denmark (which had been conquered by Germany), so it wouldn't fall into Hitler's hands. The United States also took over the defense of Iceland because Britain no longer had the resources to defend it. In August 1941, Churchill and Roosevelt met for the first time—on battleships off the coast of Newfoundland—and issued what became known as the "Atlantic Charter," a declaration of aims for peace. Then, in September, a Nazi U-boat (submarine) torpedoed a U.S. ship that had been trailing it. Roosevelt used the incident as an excuse to give the U.S. Navy an order to "shoot on sight" any German or Italian submarines it encountered while patrolling the Atlantic.

When FDR *(left)* signed a declaration of war on December 8, 1941, the United States officially entered World War II, joining Great Britain and its leader, Winston Churchill *(right)*.

Three months later, on December 7, 1941, Japan launched a surprise attack on the U.S. naval base at Pearl Harbor in Hawaii. The United States declared war on Japan. In turn, Germany and Italy—which were bound by treaty with Japan—declared war on the United States.

The United States allied itself with Great Britain. On June 22, 1941, Hitler had levied a surprise attack on the Soviet Union, breaking a pact he had signed with Stalin and sending the Soviets to the side of the Allies.

During the 27 months between the beginning of World War II and the United States' entry into it, Roosevelt sometimes took action on his own authority that should have been approved by Congress. Sometimes Roosevelt risked war by his non-neutral actions and failed to fully inform the American people of what he was doing. Sometimes he exaggerated the short-run threat the Nazis posed to the western hemisphere. Nevertheless, if some of his means were not proper, his achievements were. His role in keeping western civilization alive at this, its grimmest hour, was enormous. Winston Churchill probably summed it up the best, when he said of Roosevelt:

> Had he not acted when he did, in the way he did, [had he not] resolved to give aid to Britain and to Europe in the supreme crisis through which we have passed, a hideous fate might well have overwhelmed mankind and made its whole future for centuries sink into shame and ruin.

CHAPTER ELEVEN

Seeking a Third Term

ONE OF FDR'S MOST IMPORTANT decisions was a very personal one. In 1940, as Europe was being overrun by Hitler, the president decided to run for a third term.

When George Washington made the decision to step down after two terms as president in 1796, he set a precedent that would last nearly 150 years. Each of the two-term presidents who followed Washington—Thomas Jefferson, James Madison, James Monroe, Andrew Jackson, Ulysses Grant, Grover Cleveland, and Woodrow Wilson—did as Washington had done. Grant, who was elected in 1868 and 1872 and who did not run for reelection in 1876, did try unsuccessfully for his party's nomination again in 1880. Theodore Roosevelt, who succeeded to the presidency after William McKinley's

The 1940 Democratic National Convention in Chicago. Roosevelt was "drafted" at the convention—he received the nomination without even officially declaring his candidacy.

107

assassination in 1901 and was elected to a full term
in 1904, stepped down in 1908, but then ran unsuccessfully for the presidency as a third-party candidate
in 1912. By 1940 the "two-term" tradition was so
widely accepted that it seemed to many Americans
to be written in the Constitution.

FDR probably both did and didn't want a third
term. In 1940 he was almost 60 years old. He had
lived through two of the most difficult terms of any
president. He had a great many interests outside of
politics, and he clearly looked forward to editing his
papers, writing his memoirs and some history, and
returning to Hyde Park, where a library housing his
papers was almost complete.

On the other hand, Franklin D. Roosevelt loved
to break precedents. He had, after all, been the first
major party candidate to address a party nominating
convention in person. He had also been the first president to have a press secretary, the first to appoint
a woman to the cabinet, the first to appoint a woman
to be an ambassador. He would become the first
president to leave the United States during wartime.

Three strong arguments could be made for his
running for a third term. In the first place, he loved
being president. Second, no one in the Democratic
Party would be as strong a candidate as he would
be. If FDR didn't run, there was considerable risk
that a conservative Republican president and Congress would be elected, threatening some of the
most important New Deal programs. The third and
probably most important reason for running for
a third term was the extraordinarily grave situation
in Europe. The United States and the world required
outstanding leadership.

Roosevelt may well have waited until June 1940 to decide. Throughout 1939 and the early months of 1940, he had avoided making any statement that would completely rule him out as a candidate. Yet he also encouraged a flock of New Dealers to run for the nomination: his well-respected (though relatively conservative) secretary of state, Cordell Hull; James Farley, postmaster general and FDR's closest political adviser; Secretary of Commerce Harry Hopkins; and Senator James F. ("Jimmy") Byrnes of South Carolina. Roosevelt let each of these men think that he was the preferred choice, but he never made a commitment in public. If Roosevelt really did want the nomination himself, this was a wise strategy—it made it more difficult for any one person to clinch the nomination in advance. It also made it more difficult for those seeking his support to attack Roosevelt or his policies. There was also one strong candidate Roosevelt did not encourage because he considered him too conservative, Vice

Supporters of Republican presidential candidate Wendell Willkie believed that three terms was too long for anyone to be president.

President John Nance Garner. Of all the candidates with a real chance of receiving the nomination, Roosevelt probably preferred Hull.

In time, the presidential hopes of Hull, Farley, Hopkins, Byrnes, and Garner dimmed. Hull did not run hard for the nomination. Farley was a Catholic, and no Catholic would be elected president until John F. Kennedy took office in 1960. Hopkins suffered from chronic illness. Jimmy Byrnes, a southerner, was unlikely to run well in the northern cities, and Garner lost in primary elections. This left the way open for Roosevelt to be drafted—to receive the nomination without actually campaigning for it.

Yet Roosevelt may not have been angling for the nomination. He may not have known what he really wanted to do. In the end, the grave events in Europe may have led him to run.

On April 9, 1940, the Nazis had begun their spring offensive. Germany occupied Denmark within just two days. Norway was beaten in three weeks. Belgium and Holland were attacked on May 10. Five days later, German troops roared through France. Within a few days, the armies of France and Great Britain were driven back to the English Channel at Dunkirk. Their very survival was in doubt. France surrendered on June 21. The nominating conventions of both the Democratic and Republican Parties were less than a month away. With the American people still divided over the role the United States ought to play, Roosevelt could have honestly come to the conclusion that in such a grave crisis his talents as a leader were needed.

Indeed, on June 20, just four days before the Republican convention was to begin, Roosevelt had pulled off a remarkable coup by appointing two eminent Republicans, Henry L. Stimson and Frank Knox, secretary of war and secretary of the navy, respectively. With this move, FDR put the two departments most connected with the national defense in excellent hands. Both men felt strongly about giving assistance to Great Britain. And by appointing Republicans, Roosevelt protected himself from Republican criticism.

The Republicans nominated a strong candidate for president, Wendell Willkie. When the Democratic convention opened in Chicago on July 15, 1940, the Roosevelt supporters present included former candidates Hopkins and Burns. Yet Roosevelt himself still had not made a public statement about whether or not he wanted the nomination. However, on the second evening of the convention, Senator Alben Barkley of Kentucky said:

> Tonight, at the specific request and authorization of the President, I am making this simple fact clear to the Convention....The president has never had, and has not today, any desire or purpose to continue in the office of President....He wishes in all earnestness and sincerity to make it clear that all the delegates to the Convention are free to vote for any candidate.

A moment of silence lingered after Barkley's words. Then, from the loudspeakers around the hall came one voice, crying, "We want Roosevelt!" A few delegates started parading. Then the voice cried, "Everyone wants Roosevelt!" More delegates began parading. Finally, the voice cried, "The world wants Roosevelt!" At that, the delegates and spectators began to march. Cheerleaders, bands, and noisemakers

At the 1940 Democratic National Convention, delegates started parading about and calling, "We want Roosevelt!"

appeared, and a mob shouted "Roosevelt! Roosevelt! Roosevelt!" The voice belonged to Chicago's superintendent of sewers, Thomas F. Garry, positioned there by Chicago mayor, Edward J. Kelly, one of the most powerful Democratic leaders in the nation. Roosevelt had his draft.

The next day Roosevelt was nominated with 946 out of 1,093 votes. Farley finished second with 72. The nomination was followed by a bitter fight over the vice presidential nomination, so bitter that at one point Roosevelt seemed to be on the brink of withdrawing as the presidential candidate. He finally prevailed and his choice, Secretary of Agriculture Henry Wallace, won.

In a moving speech, the president accepted the draft:

> Only the people themselves can draft a President. If such a draft should be made upon me, I say to you, in the utmost simplicity, I will, with God's help, continue to serve with the best of my ability and with the fullness of my strength.

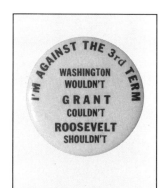

Campaign buttons such as this voiced the feelings of Willkie supporters. Despite Republican opposition, Franklin Roosevelt did win the presidency in 1940, which made him the first U.S. president to serve a third term.

During the campaign, Willkie supporters wore buttons that said, "WASHINGTON WOULDN'T. GRANT COULDN'T. ROOSEVELT SHOULDN'T." The Democrats argued that it would be "foolish to change horses in the middle of the stream." Roosevelt used what became known as the "rose garden" strategy—staying in the White House, acting "presidential," and dealing with enormously important foreign policy and defense matters. Without making political speeches, Roosevelt toured military bases, capturing public attention as commander in chief. Only in the last two weeks of the race did he openly campaign.

At the end of the campaign, in Boston, Roosevelt said words he would later regret: "I have said this before, but I shall say it again and again and again. Your boys are not going to be sent into any foreign wars."

Roosevelt won with 449 electoral votes to Willkie's 82. The president won 27,200,000 popular votes to Willkie's 22,305,000. At FDR's inauguration for his third term two months later, Chief Justice Charles Evans Hughes, waiting to administer the oath of office, turned to his old opponent from the court-packing fight and said, "Mr. President, after I have read the oath and you have repeated it, how would it do for me to lean forward and whisper, 'Don't you think this is getting a little monotonous for both of us?'"

FDR chose Secretary of Agriculture Henry Wallace *(left)* to run for the vice presidency.

Creating the United Nations

*F*RANKLIN DELANO ROOSEVELT may fairly be called the "father of the United Nations." One of his most important decisions was to try to create a permanent organization to help keep world peace and to make sure that the United States joined it.

FDR had made this a major goal of U.S. diplomacy during World War II, working hard to win public support. He had long believed that such an organization was necessary. He had served as assistant secretary of the navy in the administration of President Woodrow Wilson, who had had a similar goal. Wilson had been able to make such an organization—called the League of Nations—an important part of the Versailles Treaty, the peace settlement that ended World War I. Wilson had not been able, however, to convince the U.S. Senate to

The United Nations is housed on the east side of Manhattan, New York City, along the East River. U.N. buildings include the skyscraper on the far left; the low building along the riverfront; and the domed building.

*T*he League of Nations was founded in 1919, after World War I. It had three purposes: to maintain world peace, to settle international disputes, and to promote international cooperation. The league dissolved in 1946, transferring its services to the United Nations.

ratify the treaty, and the League of Nations came into being without the United States becoming a member. In the 1920 presidential campaign, James Cox and Franklin Roosevelt had made support for America's joining the league their central issue, but they lost the election. By the time FDR ran for president, the American people had become so strongly isolationist that he did not make membership in the league a campaign issue. And once FDR became president, he made no effort to have the United States join the league.

The league had been unable to stop Japanese, Italian, and German aggression in the 1930s—partly because it lacked American support. By the time World War II broke out in 1939, the league had lost almost all influence. It disbanded in April 1946.

Even before the United States entered World War II, Roosevelt searched for goals that would justify American support of Great Britain. In his 1941 State of the Union address, he spoke of "Four Freedoms" that the United States stood for:

The first is freedom of speech and expression—everywhere in the world.

The second is freedom of every person to worship God in his own way—everywhere in the world.

The third is freedom from want—which, translated into world terms, means economic understandings which will secure to every nation a healthy peacetime life for its inhabitants—everywhere in the world.

The fourth is freedom from fear—which, translated into world terms, means a worldwide reduction of armaments to such a point and in such a thorough fashion that no nation will be in a position to commit an act of physical aggression against any neighbor—anywhere in the world.

In August 1941, Roosevelt and Prime Minister Churchill issued the "Atlantic Charter." The goals of the charter were freedom of the seas, the right of all people to choose their own government, freedom from want, and an end to the use of force by nations.

Once the United States entered the war, Roosevelt made creation of an international peacekeeping organization a principal objective. He wanted both to inspire the American people and to insure that

This 1944 caricature shows a confident trio of FDR *(right)*, Churchill *(with cigar)*, and Stalin *(behind Churchill)* winning a domino game against Hirohito *(standing, center)*, Hitler *(seated, center)*, and Mussolini *(seated, foreground)*.

FDR at the 1943 Casablanca Conference in Morocco

after the war they would not return to isolationism. Less than a month after the attack on Pearl Harbor, on January 1, 1941, the United States, Great Britain, the Soviet Union, China, and 22 other countries issued the "United Nations Declaration," stating that they were united in the fight for the principles of the Atlantic Charter. (During the war, the name "United Nations" was simply the name of the alliance of those fighting against Germany, Japan, and Italy.)

Roosevelt's idea of the United Nations was not an organization with 25 or 50 or 75 nations with equal responsibilities. Instead, he expected that the four major nations of the alliance—the United States, Great Britain, the Soviet Union, and China—would each be most responsible for keeping the peace in its own corner of the globe and stopping the ambitions of any future Hitler. The new organization would be led by a Security Council of these greater powers.

The Council of the United Nations must have the power to act quickly and decisively to keep the peace by force, if necessary. A policeman would not be a very effective policeman if, when he saw a felon break into a house, he had to go to the Town Hall and call a town meeting to issue a warrant before the felon could be arrested....If we do not catch the international felon when we have our hands on him, if we let him get away with his loot because the Town Council has not passed an ordinance authorizing his arrest, then we are not doing our share to prevent another world war.

For the United Nations to succeed, the Soviet Union and the United States—as the two greatest powers at the end of the war—absolutely had to join.

Roosevelt made enormous efforts to persuade both countries to join. Soviet support for the new organization was first won by Secretary of State Cordell Hull during meetings in Moscow in October 1943. The United States, however, could never be sure that the suspicious Stalin wouldn't change his mind. Roosevelt continued to push for the creation of the United Nations at both of the wartime conferences with Stalin and Churchill—at Teheran at the end of 1943 and at Yalta early in 1945.

With the end of the war in sight, Roosevelt saw the United Nations as a symbol of the continuing alliance between the United States, Great Britain, and the Soviet Union. At Yalta the leaders of the three countries agreed that a conference to write a charter for a world peacekeeping organization would meet in San Francisco within three months. They also agreed on a voting formula for the new United Nations Security Council, under which each of the great powers (including China and France) would have a veto on Council action. Any subject could be brought before the Council. To satisfy Stalin, who said he was afraid of being ganged up on by all the Western nations, the Soviets were awarded three votes (out of more than 10) in the General Assembly of the United Nations. Every other nation would have only one vote.

Roosevelt was not just anxious for the Soviet Union and Britain to join the United Nations. He was also concerned about whether or not the United States would join. He remembered President Wilson's mistakes, and was successful in not repeating them. Unlike Wilson, he made certain that leading Republicans were asked for advice and support. He also made sure that congressional leaders of both parties supported the creation of the United Nations. In November 1943, with the help of Secretary of State Hull, the Roosevelt administration was able to get a resolution through the Senate (which would have to ratify the U.N. charter) by a vote of 85 to 5. The resolution committed the United States to membership in a future organization for peace.

In April 1944, a committee of eight senators from both parties was created to consult with the administration on matters of foreign policy. Many meetings were held that smoothed the path for

The United Nations

When the Allied powers founded the United Nations in 1945, they hoped an international peace-keeping organization would prevent future world wars. The 51 original members agreed to maintain international peace and security, develop friendly relations among nations, and cooperate in solving international problems. Since then, the United Nations has grown to more than twice its original size.

Its agencies include the United Nations Children's Fund (UNICEF), the United Nations Educational, Scientific, and Cultural Organization (UNESCO), and the International Bank for Reconstruction and Development (the World Bank). The U.N. also includes the International Court of Justice (the World Court), which helps to settle disputes between nations.

favorable Senate action. When Roosevelt appointed an eight-person delegation to the San Francisco conference, he named four members of Congress—two from each party—as well as a Republican state governor and an independent, Virginia Gildersleeve, the Dean of Barnard College, and Cordell Hull himself (although he had stepped down as secretary of state because of his health).

On March 1, 1945, Roosevelt spoke to Congress about the Yalta meetings. During the previous few months, his health had deteriorated. He was so weak that for the first time, he addressed the Congress sitting down. Roosevelt spoke about the conference in San Francisco that was scheduled to begin in eight weeks.

> No plan is perfect. Whatever is adopted at San Francisco will doubtless have to be amended time and again over the years, just as our own Constitution has been. No one can say exactly how long any plan will last. Peace can endure only so long as humanity really insists upon it, and is willing to work for it and sacrifice for it.

The Charter of the United Nations was ratified by the Senate 89 to 2. On October 24, 1945, the United States was the first nation to ratify the Charter.

CHAPTER THIRTEEN

A Nation Mourns

*T*HROUGH MUCH OF HIS PRESI-
dency, Roosevelt was in excellent health—
except for a sinus condition. After he returned
home from the Teheran meeting with Churchill
and Stalin in November 1943, however, his health
declined sharply. A heavy smoker (four packs a day),
disabled, and relatively inactive (he had less time to
exercise during the war), Roosevelt began to suffer
from heart disease, hypertension, hardening of the
arteries, and pulmonary disease.

By 1944, the work of the president—reading
reports, seeing people, making decisions—that had
been so easy for him for so many years—now ex-
hausted him. His great zest for life lessened. By 1944
he was a lonely man. A number of his old friends

FDR's health had declined a great deal by the time he met with
Churchill *(seated, left)* and Stalin *(seated, right)* at Yalta in 1945.

and advisers had died. His four sons were serving in the armed services far away.

Roosevelt's diplomatic, political, and military abilities did not seem to be greatly affected by his health—at least not until the last few months of his life. Nevertheless, he should not have run for a fourth term in 1944. This time his running mate was Senator Harry Truman of Missouri. His opponent was Governor Thomas E. Dewey of New York. The Roosevelt-Truman ticket won easily.

Although a heart specialist saw Roosevelt daily for more than a year, never once did Roosevelt want

A weary FDR was greeted by Winston Churchill at the 1945 Yalta Conference.

to know about his own health. Undoubtedly, he wanted desperately to see the war through to the end and to help fashion the peace. He probably could not face the news that this might not be possible. He seemed to muster enough energy to participate ably at the Yalta conference, but after his return home he became "a ghost of a great statesman" whose subordinates handled diplomatic matters in his name.

During his last year in office, Roosevelt took several vacations that helped him keep going. At the end of March 1945, he left Washington for his retreat at Warm Springs, Georgia. Early in the afternoon of Thursday, April 12, Roosevelt suddenly put his hand to his forehead and said softly, "I have a terrific headache." His hand fell and he slumped to his left. Although he received medical attention immediately, the president died without regaining consciousness two hours and twenty minutes later. He had suffered a massive brain hemorrhage.

Vice President Harry Truman was called urgently to the White House. Eleanor Roosevelt gave him the news at a little after 5:00 P.M. Winston Churchill was informed in his study in London and sat stunned for a long time. In Moscow, Ambassador Averell Harriman drove to the Kremlin at two in the morning to tell Stalin.

Throughout the United States men and women wept. Many felt what a navy seaman voiced:

When Harry Truman found out that FDR had died and he himself would become president, he told reporters "the whole weight of the moon and stars" had fallen on him.

> You know it's tough when one of your buddies has to go, and President Roosevelt was our buddy. He died in active service, just as much as any GI whose number came up in a foxhole.

Running for a Fourth Term

FDR told person after person that he did not want to run for a fourth term. His health had declined. He was often heard to say,

"All that is within me cries to go back to my home on the Hudson River." With the war still raging, however, FDR may have been reluctant to subject the country to the transition to a new administration. When Republicans—who nominated New York Governor Thomas Dewey—charged that 16 years was too long for anyone to be president, Roosevelt responded by saying that the United States should not "change horses in mid-stream."

Roosevelt's body was taken by railroad from Warm Springs to Washington. As the train made its way through the cotton fields and tobacco farms of Georgia, South Carolina, and North Carolina, people waited along the tracks to offer a final salute. Thousands waited in the larger cities.

The train arrived in Washington on the morning of April 14. The casket was placed on a caisson and, to the muffled roll of drums, carried to the White House by six white horses through streets lined with crowds.

The funeral service was held in the White House—in the East Room where Lincoln had also lain. Among the mourners were Edith Wilson (the widow of Woodrow Wilson), retired Chief Justice Charles Evans Hughes, and FDR's final election opponent, Governor Thomas Dewey of New York. When the minister closed his prayer, he paused and quoted from the first inaugural—"Let me assert my firm belief that the only thing we have to fear is fear itself."

That night FDR's funeral train left for Hyde Park, passing through Philadelphia and New York, and then rolling north along Roosevelt's beloved Hudson River. When the train arrived at Hyde Park on the morning of April 15, violets were in bloom, although a cold wind blew. Roosevelt was buried as he wished, in his mother's rose garden, behind the house where he was born.

"A Strong and Active Faith"

Not every one of FDR's decisions was wise. After the attack on Pearl Harbor, Roosevelt approved the decision to evict Japanese Americans from their homes and have them placed in internment camps for the duration of the war. Although FDR did issue an executive order requiring desegregation of plants doing business with the government during the war, he could have worked harder to assist African Americans. And Roosevelt made less of an effort than he should have to allow Jewish refugees from Europe into the United States. This might have saved hundreds of thousands of lives.

Nevertheless, whenever historians rank U.S. presidents, Roosevelt is always among the top three, along with Washington and Lincoln. Washington set the course for the United States, while Lincoln saw it through its greatest test—the Civil War. Franklin

Churchill and FDR *(both seated)* at a strategy-planning conference in North Africa.

Delano Roosevelt led the nation through two enormous crises: a devastating Depression and a world war. He served as president longer than anyone else.

Roosevelt was the person in the United States most responsible for creating a system of welfare. Believing that government existed to serve the general welfare of all the people, Roosevelt used the power of the federal government to help those in need. "The test of our progress," he said, "is not whether we add more to the abundance of those who have much; it is whether we provide enough for those who have too little." The role of the federal government was greatly enlarged during Roosevelt's presidency,

From his tough stand as the United States' leader in international affairs, to his undertaking in compassion for all Americans, FDR left a powerful legacy for presidents to follow.

creating a large federal bureaucracy. "Better," he once said, "the occasional faults of a government that lives in a spirit of charity than the constant omissions of a Government frozen in the ice of its own indifference."

Roosevelt also persuaded the American people to shoulder the responsibilities befitting a great power. He led them to victory during World War II and made sure that after the war they would continue to accept responsibility for the preservation of world peace. The western world might well have not survived without the aid Roosevelt gave to Great Britain in 1940 and 1941. As commander in chief,

Roosevelt chose the generals and admirals who developed strategies for successful campaigns in North Africa, Europe, and the Pacific. Roosevelt was also responsible for the brilliant national effort to produce weapons, not only for the United States, but also for its allies. Roosevelt fulfilled Woodrow Wilson's dream of U.S. participation in an international peacekeeping organization.

Roosevelt has been a tremendous influence on all his successors as president. Under Roosevelt, American citizens have come to view the workings of their government in terms of the actions of the president. Roosevelt was the first president who understood the opportunities for leadership through the use of radio and press conferences. Roosevelt created the modern White House staff. And more

NDS & STAMPS *NOW*

FDR encouraged Americans to believe in their country and in themselves.

than any other president, Roosevelt was responsible for the expectation that a strong president will dominate the Congress.

Finally, Roosevelt created a nation free of fear. He had the talent to "rekindle our spirits in times of despair." When democracy was threatened, first by economic collapse and then by Hitler, Roosevelt never lost his nerve. Calm and confident, Roosevelt had no doubt and left no doubt that America would persevere. In a speech he had planned to give on April 13, 1945, Roosevelt would have urged the American people to "do all in our power to conquer the doubts and the fears, the ignorance and the greed." That speech would have concluded: "The only limit to our realization of tomorrow will be our doubts of today. Let us move forward with strong and active faith."

Perhaps no president of the United States has left more of a mark than Franklin Delano Roosevelt. The impact of Roosevelt can still be seen in dams, roads, and schools built by the Public Works Administration; in forests reclaimed by the Civil Conservation Corps; and in murals painted by artists working for other New Deal agencies. Roosevelt's legacy can be seen in mandatory minimum wages and better working conditions, in mandatory retirement pensions, and in unemployment insurance. It can be seen not only in the strength of labor unions but also in the strength of free enterprise in the United States. It can be seen in America's structure of alliances throughout the world and in the United Nations. And he left something more—the spirit of a man who had supreme confidence in democracy and in the good the United States government could do, not only for its own people, but for those all around the world.

FDR's presidency left a lasting impact on the American way of life.

Index

Knox, Frank, 110

League of Nations, 115–116
Lend-Lease Act, 103
Lincoln, Abraham, 10, 58, 127, 129
Lippmann, Walter, 31

Marshall, George, 49
Mercer, Lucy, 23
Moley, Raymond, 43–44
Moore, A. Henry, 77
Mussolini, Benito, 36, 37, 117

National Governor's Conference, 72
National Industrial Recovery Act, 66
National Labor Relations Act, 83, 87
Nazi Party, of Germany, 33, 37
Neutrality Acts, 92, 95
New Deal, 66, 68–69, 82–83, 87
New Deal, Second, 75–76, 79
Nixon, Richard, 10, 68

Office of the President, 49

Perkins, Francis, 74, 75
Poland, 95–97
president, 8–9
    decision making, 9–11, 47
    powers of, 68
    staff of, 48–49, 130
Price Control Act, 52
Public Works Administration, 66, 132

Robinson, Joseph, 88
Roosevelt, Eleanor, 23, 24, 27, 45, 50, 51, 125
    as aide to the president, 50–51
Roosevelt, Franklin D.
    as assistant secretary of the navy, 25–26,
        27, 31
    attempted assassination of, 29
    birth of, 21
    campaign for president (1932), 28, 42–45
    campaign for president (1940), 106–107,
        111–113
    campaign for president (1944), 126
    childhood of, 22–23
    criticisms of, 74–75, 84–87, 127
    death of, 125
    and the decision-making process, 47–53

decisions
    about aid to Great Britain, 91–105
    about the Great Depression, 63–69
    about running for a fourth term, 126
    about running for a third term, 107–113
    about Social Security, 71–79
    about the Supreme Court, 81–89
    about the United Nations, 115–121
    education of, 23
    elected president. *See* elections of 1932, 1936,
        1940, 1944
    end of presidency, 125–127
    fireside chats, 57–58, 64–65, 95, 102
    "firsts" as president, 108
    as governor of New York, 27, 28, 29, 30,
        42–43
    health, decline of, 123–125
    inauguration of 1933, 13, 18–19, 63, 82
    inauguration of 1937, 56
    marriage of, 23
    military career of, 25–26
    New Deal, 66, 68–69, 132
    personality and qualities of, 55–61
    and polio, 23, 27, 61
    political principles of, 41–45
    politics, entry into, 23–24
    press conferences, 56–57, 130
    qualifications for presidency, 30–31
    relationship with Congress, 64, 66, 130
    as senator of New York State, 24, 27
    vice president of the U.S., candidate for,
        26, 27
    welfare, creation of, 129
    White House staff, 48–49, 130
Roosevelt, James, 20–21
Roosevelt, Sara Delano, 20–21, 22–23
Roosevelt, Theodore, 23–25, 42, 45, 55, 107
Russia. *See* Soviet Union
Rutledge, Wiley, 89

Securities Act, 67
Smith, Al, 27–28, 29
Snell, Bertrand, 52
Social Security Act, 71–79, 83, 87
Soviet Union, 35, 94–96, 105, 117–119
Stalin, Joseph, 35–36, 69, 105, 117, 125
    meeting with Roosevelt, 119, 122–123
Stimson, Henry L., 110
Supreme Court, U.S., 9, 81–89

Acknowledgments

Photographs reproduced with permission of: The White House, pp. 2–3; Independence National Historical Park, pp. 6–7; Independent Picture Service, pp. 8–9 *(below, all)*, 11 *(both)*, 40–41, 52, 53, 68, 76, 104 *(right)*; National Archives, pp. 8 *(top)*, 12–13 *(306-NT-165.319c)*, 16–17 *(83-G-41563)*, 32–33 *(W + C #989)*, 37 *(W + C #746)*, 48 *(59-JB-HULL-5)*, 60 *(69-RP-1L-2)*, 61 *(79-AR-145c)*, 62–63 *(306-NT-157.062c)*, 78 *(69-N-17200)*, 93 *(W + C #982)*, 97 *(306-PS-51-9773)*, 104 *(left, 79-AR-82)*, 128 *(W + C #748)*; *Employment Agency* by Isaac Soyer, 1937, collection of the Whitney Museum of American Art, p. 14; Library of Congress, pp. 15, 56, 66, 75, 86, 102, 125; Franklin D. Roosevelt Library, pp. 18, 20–21, 22, 23, 24, 26 (Army War College), 27, 29, 44, 50, 58 (U.S. Office of War Information), 59, 64, 67, 70–71, 74, 109, 112, 117, 118, 122–123, 124, 126, 129, 132, back cover; Art Resource, NY, p. 30; USASC, p. 36; Bureau of Engraving, Washington, D.C., p. 42; UPI/Bettmann, pp. 46–47, 54–55, 57, 80–81, 82, 100, 103, 106–107, 111, 113, 130–131; Dwight D. Eisenhower Library, p. 49; Minneapolis Public Library and Information Center, p. 51; The Bettmann Archive, pp. 73, 88; The Supreme Court Historical Society, p. 85; U.S. Army, pp. 90–91; Fitzpatrick in the *St. Louis Post-Dispatch*, photo courtesy of State Historical Society of Missouri, Columbia, p. 94; United Nations, pp. 114–115, 120.